BEGGAR

BEE

NAMELESS

Beggar Bee Nameless

By Stephen K Easterbrook

© Stephen K Easterbrook

ISBN: 9781912092451

First published in 2023

Published by Palavro, an imprint of
the Arkbound Foundation (Publishers)

Arkbound is a social enterprise that aims to promote social inclusion, community development and artistic talent. It sponsors publications by disadvantaged authors and covers issues that engage wider social concerns. Arkbound fully embraces sustainability and environmental protection. It endeavours to use material that is renewable, recyclable or sourced from sustainable forest.

Arkbound
Rogart Street Campus
4 Rogart Street
Glasgow, G40 2AA

www.arkbound.com

BEGGAR

BEE

STEPHEN K EASTERBROOK

NAMELESS

palavro
PUBLISHING

To Maggie and Andrew

To you who have no home
No room to call your own
To you who walk the streets
And have no bed in which to sleep
To you who left the strife
Of that sorry other life
To you who have no clue
On how or what to do
We offer up this humble code
For getting by on the beggar's road.

One: never bum from a bum
Two: beggars can't be choosers
Three: God bless the Muggles
Four: clean kids are mean kids
Five: there is safety in numbers
Six: eat or be worm's meat
Seven: a newspaper is an insulator
Eight: layers are saviours
Nine: give use to the useless
Ten: a shark is a wolf is a shark
Eleven: trust not the Gimps
Twelve: shelter from life

– The Beggar's Code

THE NAMELESS

Shane Ellis studied the picture on her phone. It was a curious fact that she never saw bodies in the course of her work. A corpse was removed promptly from its scene of discovery and long before any DAO took charge. Sometimes decay left its mark if the remains had lain in a residence for some time. There could be the smell of putrefaction when she opened the door, or a telltale stain on the departed's mattress, from which the sheets had been stripped and taken for burning. But her only sight of the Nameless was the photo which came with the casefile, grim or peaceful, taken on the coroner's slab. The one on her phone that morning was of a homeless man who had died of exposure.

A great many of her customers were homeless as itineracy went hand in hand with effaced tracks and disembodied pasts. If they were immigrants, it made things 20 times harder because it meant partnering with foreign agencies. This cadaver was of a white person, though impossible to say whether he was from these shores, or even Manchester itself. The hair was dark and curly, the face stubbled, not bearded, and the cheeks were noticeably sunken, though whether in death or from malnutrition, it was impossible to tell. A single distinguishing feature per the pathologist's report: the thumb of his right hand was missing. Not amputated recently, and a clean cut rather than some industrial tear. It lacked the nice suturing of a medical procedure.

A passerby had found him, wrapped in a sleeping bag, under the sheltered entrance to one of the buildings from Manchester's Victorian past: a grade II listed exchange on the corner of Oldham

Street. Its limestone had browned from the pollution since its heyday, and the windows were arched and tightly packed above their ornamental ledges. A single turret crowned the place, five floors up from where the man had bedded down for the final night of his life.

It was busy there, being a confluence of the city's arteries and its transport hub. People of all types arrived at Piccadilly Station, trekked down the slope and made their way along Market Street to the Arndale. Trams from all corners of the Greater Manchester area were sucked into this debouching point. Not far away lay the hipster, up-and-coming Northern Quarter and the vibrant Chinatown. She couldn't think of a crisper embodiment of modern Mancunian existence: the emblem of the city was the worker bee, and this was a hive.

Opening the door on a life was a skill. There was no checklist of inquiry for a DAO. Irrespective of photos provided, Shane would always visit the spot where a nameless had been recovered. If you saw how someone had died, then you might understand how they'd lived; walk in their shoes, and you might learn who they were during daylight, and in the night time too.

Along Oldham Street people gathered in the bus shelters. They hunched under the cold of a working day, eyes drawn to mobiles, oblivious to her purpose and the death which had brought her there.

What do they think of the Homeless? she wondered. Deserving of pity and charity? Layabouts who would rather beg than take a job?

Likely they saw them as a collective. The Homeless. The things that the Homeless held in common were what made them different from the Homed. They spoke and acted in a particular way, with their grimy, wrinkled faces; they slept under newspapers and in cardboard boxes. Their life was a life apart from the appreciated norms. Their day was the opposite of everything that the Homed might cherish and pursue: stability, security, warmth. It was easy to set the Homeless at a remove. To imagine they didn't think or feel the same as others.

The DAO kept going, past cafés, office buildings, an arts and crafts store. Her eyes scanned the pavements. At the next junction, a homeless man was sat in front of a Tesco Metro.

'I know the face,' he said at length, squinting at the picture. He shifted uneasily. 'Bit creepy that. Photo of a dead body on yer phone.'

It was not the first time she had walked the streets of Manchester this way, trying to get information from other rough sleepers who might have known a deceased, but it was a population in constant flux. She rarely met the same person twice, and it was potluck whether one vagrant had known another when alive. She felt a prickle of excitement.

'You knew him. What was his name?'

'Dunno. Just seen him 'round. That's all.'

A hot chocolate mocha had been her way into the conversation, a mocha with three white sugars delivered separately in their packets for him to use as he wanted. Two got poured into the cup, and his thick hands daintily gripped the stirrer; the third went into the pouch of his rucksack. Soon foam rested happily on his top lip. When he spoke again, she saw how few teeth remained, and that they were rotten at the gumline.

'What does it matter now? Won't be bothering no one no more. Not now he's a Mr Freeze.'

'How old was he?'

'You one of the Gimps?'

'No,' she said. 'Gimps' was slang for Greater Manchester Police, after their acronym, GMP.

'Trust not the Gimps,' he said mysteriously as his eyes twinkled.

'I work for the council. I'm a Deceased Affairs officer.'

He shook a sad head. 'Was just a kid. Eighteen, nineteen. Somethin' like that.'

'The thumb on his right hand was missing.'

'Ah. Probably got on the wrong side of... people.' A quick glance around. 'The side that want their bread back. With interest.'

'He owed money?'

'Wouldn't be the first. There's plenny got thumbs missin' in this city.'

Her gaze journeyed to the man's hands, but all the digits were there: no abrupt endings at the joints.

'Payment-in-kind,' he murmured, as she produced some coins and walked on.

The Mancunian rain began to fall, with that firm hand which signifies it will be there for hours, and the DAO retraced her steps to the Gardens, opening the compact umbrella that she always carried with her. There was a tram stop 50 yards off, by the Primark at the top of Market Street, and she headed for it.

With few qualifications to speak of, Shane had gone straight into her job from school. She knew that being a Deceased Affairs officer, or 'DAO', made her sound like some second-rate detective, that generic descriptions like 'council worker' or 'civil servant' were more palatable in polite company than the morbid reality. There could be no pretensions about her role. She was simply a tidier, an administrator of finalities. She tied up the loose ends of another being's end when there was no one but the state to do so.

And yet, the fate of the Nameless had always mattered to Shane. There was something compelling about the study of concluded lives when no one came forward to claim a body. It was poignant to see the line of oblivion so close at hand, where death could mean effacement, complete and categoric, from the world's memory. It made her think of her own departure: the mourning of others, the remembrance of a life, the questions of legacy and estate. In death people deserved a name, the name their mother gave them. And sometimes a DAO could return it.

This Nameless had died with a number of possessions. There

were photos in the case file, and Shane studied them as the tram wheels scraped along the rails, rocking and jarring at the turns. They were the items that any streetsleeper might have: a small duffel bag of clothes; newspaper scraps; a penknife; lengths of twine; and a handful of donated notes and coins. Other objects were less expected: a toothbrush and toothpaste; a razor and shaving foam; a comb and small mirror. He might well have been a tramp, but he'd not been trampish.

Finally, there was a small, white plastic box, with a rubber band holding its middle. It had been kept in a sealed bag. Inside the box, the police had found a strip of red card with a gold filigree border and flourishes. It looked like one half of a bookmark torn in two. On it was printed the first line of that famous couplet from *Romeo and Juliet*:

What's in a name? That which we call a rose...

As Shane looked out of the tram window, she considered the quiet irony of that message from beyond the grave. Its mysterious nature, too. Like the missing thumb, it was a piece of the unknown, no less than the name itself.

The tram waited 10 minutes at a stop. The weather persisted. Two large raindrops, starting from opposite corners of Shane's window, began their journeys down its freckled surface. As she watched, they turned towards each other. Other beads moved, shook and slid under the vibration of the idling engine, but none disrupted the pair that were made for one another. They came together in the heart of the window and sped to the bottom.

The nameless had wanted the box to be waterproof, she thought. For the moment it was unclear why he'd preserved the torn bookmark, and it might well stay that way, but it had clearly mattered to him a great deal.

GRACIE

'He used to hang around with a young woman. Her name was Gracie.'

'Was?'

'She died of a drug overdose. About a year ago.'

The woman speaking was in her early 40s, with a bob cut that bounced with compulsive energy when she spoke. Shane had known Karen for a good six or seven years now, as Deceased Affairs meant regular contact with members of the homeless support network. Karen was a senior assistant at Hope Mission, a charitable foundation in the Northern Quarter which offered food, shelter and care to the rough-sleeping community.

'It was Spice, as I remember. Well, not the Spice itself, but something it was cut with.'

About 18 months before, Manchester had become headline news up and down the country for the Spice habit which was plaguing its city centre. Scores of 'zombies', rendered catatonic under its effects, were seen slumped against walls, bus shelters and park benches, or doubled over impossibly at the waist, feet rooted to the middle of the High Street, for hour after hour. Unkind souls had made videos and uploaded them to social media. The problem had peaked, but the images persisted in the city's memory, a blot on its standing as a hub of new investment and cosmopolitan sensibilities.

'Dealers used to cut the Spice with brodifacoum,' said Karen. 'It adds to the high, but it's basically rat poison. We've known a lot die that way.'

'What do you know about the young man?'

She sighed. 'Very little, I'm afraid.'

Some cases gave up their secrets with ease while others remained mute and intractable. A third type never made up their mind, mixing opportune breakthroughs with cruel disappointments. Shane had been to several shelters before Hope Mission, but this was the first place where anyone had recognised the nameless. Her hopes rose that his details might have been 'processed', but Karen knew nothing of his name or background and nothing of a family who could be contacted for funeral arrangements. He was from the Manchester area, she believed, 'like Gracie.' He'd appeared on the streets a couple of years before. He was in his teens, just as the mocha-drinking vagrant had speculated.

'I knew Gracie better,' she said. 'She wrote the Beggar's Code, you see.'

'The Beggar's Code?'

'Yes. It's a set of rules. Or maybe principles. How to live on the streets. Hang on...' Karen rooted through the drawers of her desk, and then the filing cabinet behind her. 'I have a copy... which I read now and again. It helps remind me that, sometimes, the Homeless see life quite differently to us. Here.'

She brought out an A5 laminated card with a short poem on one side and a curious list on the other, all handwritten. The Beggar's Code. The DAO turned it in her hands, quietly absorbed.

'It was popular for a time. Especially with people who'd just arrived on the streets. Gave them some kind of starting point, from someone who understood what they were going through. We stocked copies of it with our other leaflets and flyers. It was funny seeing all those government pamphlets untouched while the code flew out the door. We asked her to come and talk about the rules and her experiences – here, in our little meeting room. They were well attended. Then things went a bit sour.'

'How come?'

'The council didn't like the code. They felt it promoted begging instead of encouraging people off the streets and back into housing. Which is right, I get it – I mean look how these poor kids ended up. Anyway, the council said it wasn't a message they supported, so we had to stop the talks.'

Shane knew the majority of charity funding came from grants applied for through the council. Her boss signed off on many annually. Hope Mission would have had little choice.

She took a picture of the laminated card and handed it back. 'Thank you.'

'The stuff around not trusting the police wasn't well received either.' She grinned, and the bob cut danced again. 'I heard that Gracie still gave some talks on the streets, but then it all went quiet. She'd gone away, someplace else. The next I knew she'd already passed, a couple of months or more, and I hadn't even known. The Street moves on so fast. It's a terrible thing, Shane. These youngsters dying with their whole lives in front of them. We try, but it's never enough.'

The DAO believed that the roots of such tragedies lay in childhoods gone wrong. Per the life stories she uncovered, the Homeless shared more than a lack of home. They shared pre-street miseries.

Whatever her sorrows as an adult, Shane had been a happy, nurtured child. Born to two teachers with steady if not stellar incomes, she was never the victim of too little money, nor a casualty of too much, and her family had been ordinary in that beneficial way: her sister was the academic, her brother the joker; she'd respected her father and vexed her mother. Throughout there'd been a stable home, and she'd never contemplated otherwise. It was beyond the margins of imagination, an unrehearsed fear. Even now Shane struggled to picture how it must be: the forlorn nights, a cutthroat Street, the cold in your bones, and a hustle for survival.

'The young man,' she began, 'the pathologist's report said the thumb of his right hand was missing.'

'Ah, yes.' Karen nodded, as though a memory had been triggered. 'I saw him a couple of times after Gracie died, from a distance. He took it bad. You could tell. Then I saw him a few months back. When he came into the soup canteen, I noticed his thumb was missing. He seemed... it's strange, he seemed better after that. Like he'd turned a corner. He laughed at something one of the others said, while he was stood in line. Really struck me at the time, given the loss of his thumb. I guess grief is like that, though.'

The Deceased Affairs officer agreed quietly. She had experienced the pain of terrible loss herself, the twists and turns that grief took, the search for catharsis. Her hand clenched under the table.

'What about Gracie's surname? Family?'

The charity worker shook her head. 'I spoke with her a couple of times. Some rough sleepers open up but not her. I got the impression there was a dark history there, darker than most. Other members of the community might know. There was an old man she used to hang around with too, though I haven't seen him for a long time.' She considered. 'Speak with Darren. He knew Gracie. And he gives talks now, like she did, only a toned-down version. No code. Just his experiences.'

'Darren?' She wrote the name down.

'Yes. He's speaking here tomorrow.'

Shane glanced at her watch. She had a doctor's appointment and did not want to be late. Having thanked Karen, she returned to the streets.

The tram wound its way slowly through the city she called home. Founded at the join between the Medlock and the Irwell, Manchester was bequeathed by the Romans to the Saxons, then by the Saxons to the Danes; the pattern of their tenures could be seen still in the crooks of certain streets, and in their ancient, perpetuating labels – Deansgate, Millgate – like distilleries of history. During the 19th century, when the Industrial Revolution was in full swing, she became the boldest flower in that brooding, urgent display. Manchester was home to the world's first passenger railway station, gave the glorious Ship Canal its name, pioneered coal transport and the new wharf constructions. The boom had created wealth, and the deepest of poverties too. They persisted today.

From her window Shane watched the moving figures. They were a tough people, the Mancunians, gruff in tongue and sarcastic of wit, friendly without being mugs, bees of a bitter honey. The Beggar's Code came to mind once more, and with it a peculiar, civic pride, as she remembered those mildly cryptic lines, penned by a young woman she had never met, but who was a daughter of the city and now beneath its ground. 'Never bum from a bum', 'beggars can't be choosers', 'give use to the useless'. These were rules for more than the Homeless. There was a deeper creed there. I wonder what Gracie was like, the DAO thought to herself. She tried to conjure a picture of how the young woman might have looked, but no image came; suddenly the tram had reached her stop.

WORKER BEE

Ryan squeezed Shane's hand lightly as they sat on one of the upholstered benches in the waiting room. She returned the squeeze and did her best to smile. But as she sat there the lie that she had been spinning for months lay heavily across her chest, rounding her shoulders, constricting her breath. She wore a contraceptive cap when she and her husband had sex, without him knowing. She removed it after; flushed any sperm down the toilet. Shane found herself at the centre of a knot of contradictions: she desperately wanted a child, but simply could not bear the thought of one. She didn't want the old grief resolved. She couldn't risk a new grief beginning. She wanted time, and all associated feeling, to stop.

The doctor called them into the consulting room. There was a revolving stool and desk for the doctor, an examination bed and two chairs for patient and companion. To Shane's left, as she sat, was a large sash window whose glass shone in the afternoon sun. Outside, the wheels of a pushchair clattered on the flagstones as a young mother arrived at the surgery entrance. The baby cried and Shane's mouth tensed.

A squirrel appeared outside the sash window. Slick and intrepid, it nipped along a tree branch before scaling a drainpipe. Its black eye locked on Shane, round as a button. As she stared back, she registered the animalistic nature of the blackness, the kind which shifts between fullness and emptiness, between vacancy and knowing, in the tick of a clock. The flashes of absence were the most disturbing, for it felt like the creature peered right through her and apprehended the guilt in her heart.

'You've been trying for a baby for the last 12 months,' the doctor began, 'I can't see anything physically wrong with you, from the various test results. Sometimes, in cases like yours, fertility rates can be affected – it's not a significant percentage, but it can happen. It might make sense for me to refer you for IVF at this stage, if that's what you'd like to do. You're entitled to three rounds of treatment on the NHS.'

Ryan gave her a rub on the shoulder which made her tingle with shame. They probably didn't need IVF, if she'd remove her contraception. She didn't know what she would do now. IVF created embryos for embedding in the womb, which might or might not take. She felt the waters rising around her.

'I'm working on a very important case at the moment,' she said, instantly feeling stupid for saying it. The doctor had been typing up a note. She glanced up at this.

The woman had a white, Moomin-like face, and a sharp fringe which emphasised the roundness and blankness. Years of GP work had deadened her reactions to pretty much any statement, so she merely said, 'It will take a little time for the IVF referral to be processed in any case.'

As they left the surgery, Shane noticed a pile of leaflets among the usual literature by the exit. Its title was Spice Warning, and the subtitle: Information about Recent Incidents Involving Spice in Manchester. Its incongruity shone in the genteel surroundings of the middle-class medical practice, away from the urban holes where the drug had its grip; she bent and took the leaflet with her.

It was hard having a normal evening at home after such an appointment. They danced around the subject for some time, mirroring their evasion in the way they pushed their food around the plates.

Finally, he spoke. 'Tell me about this case you mentioned.'

She looked at Ryan. He would have made a good father. He

was a good, kind husband. It might be a cliché, but didn't men bury their feelings in these situations? It was true they hadn't talked about it much, but then what was there to say? Mourning was such an individualistic act. There was no 'code' for that. When Shane's father had died seven years ago, the gathered had talked memories, and that was all – there were tears of course, but no existential chats or wholesale unburdening about what it meant, and how sorrow should unfold. There were no memories to chew over with this bereavement. No structure to hang the grief on. And so, the focus had shifted after a few months to ploughing away at another conception.

'What's that, love?'

'You mentioned you were on a case.'

'Yes. A young homeless guy. He was found in the city centre, off Piccadilly Gardens. It was exposure.'

'How old?'

'Late teens.'

'That's awful.' He paused. 'Listen. I know you have to work through all that. But with the IVF, well I'm here, my support's here, when you need.'

'Thanks.' For a moment she swayed. It was on the tip of her tongue to tell him about the contraception; she knew it was wrong to deceive him. But she just really, really, could not.

'That's alright.' He picked up his plate and hers. 'I'll stack the dishwasher.'

She sat on the bed upstairs. It was all too painful. She could see her face in the mirror, and she let her eyes meet those in the reflection.

A floorboard creaked. Ryan was in the doorway. He sat beside her on the bed, gently touched her arm and back. She held his hand. A minute later she excused herself and went to the bathroom briefly, then returned.

'Try one more time?' he asked.

Afterwards, Shane removed the cap. She closed the lid of

the loo and stayed there; this time she really cried, muffling the sounds with a towel so as not to wake Ryan. She let the tears stream from her eyes.

In the moment of calm that followed, a picture came into her head: sharp, striking, clear as day. A worker bee: that emblem of tireless industry, of unswerving execution, of communal commitment and collective delivery. Its yellow body was bold and beautiful; its wings were iridescent pearls. There was something to hold onto in that elegant cipher, a ballast among the turbulence, a vision of doing and being, of obligation and role. Like the bee, Shane had a duty, and hers was to the non-living, in whatever nuanced state they might be. It was more than a matter of names. It was about the restoration of dignity. They had no voice; they could not help themselves. They needed her careful, relentless diligence – to find a relative, to secure a send-off.

As she lay in bed, a renewed sense of significance washed over her, building from her stomach, and she went to sleep thinking of the young, thumbless man who had died in Piccadilly Gardens, and of her duty to him.

LEGACY

The man called Darren stood in the Hope Mission meeting room and waited for the audience to gather. He was wiry and carried himself with confidence. He looked in robust health. There was no sign of the usual toll that a life of vagrancy exacted, but that in itself was an advertisement for the speech he was about to give.

Shane had arrived before anyone else and taken a seat at the back of the room. She watched as he cleared his throat and began. There was something curious about him, this veteran of the Street. His voice modulated across two or more regional accents so she struggled to place his origin. He wore a suit, but the first thing he did was to remove his jacket and roll up his sleeves, revealing the tattoo of a lion sprawled across his forearm. His stance was open, and he spoke with ease, but his gaze travelled without ever resting on another's, as though he'd learned long ago not to seek eye contact.

It took about two minutes to spot the similarities between his talk and the Beggar's Code. The DAO bridled inwardly on behalf of the dead woman, Gracie, as Darren gave her no credit. His was a less controversial version than hers, with no critique of the authorities and an epilogue to say that he'd now found accommodation. That, he added compliantly, should be the ultimate goal of any vagrant.

The few women of the group seemed to hang on his every word. Shane sensed, in a mysterious and slightly perturbing form, the power that he might exercise over them should he wish. It made her wonder what his relationship with Gracie had been.

As she shifted in her seat, she felt the awkward edge of the Spice leaflet that she'd picked up in the doctor's waiting room the day before. Unconsciously she took it from her pocket.

There was a section on harm reduction advice for prospective Spice users, which included laughable lines like, 'Sit down before you smoke Spice as you may lose your balance', and for any well-heeled Samaritan who might chance upon a sufferer, 'Look after people who have overdosed in the same way you would want them to look after you.'

It served to underline a difficult social truth. The world was split in two, and a chasm of understanding rose between the halves. There were the tramps she had spoken to the day before, the tales of privation written on their features, the young corpse with its thumb missing and Gracie perishing at an age no person should. Then there was everybody else, herself included: that great majority who had four walls around them and a roof above, warmth and protection from the elements. Their sole bond to the former was a patronising spirit, a clumsy empathy, a gripe of pity. The leaflet was useless, other than its ability to represent that enormous divide.

The divide was there in the room too. Most of the audience were destitute, and most of them were debutants on the streets, destined for God knew what experience. What did she, or any proxy for the housed contingent, know of that predicament?

Shane knew about process. She knew the state used prioritisation by classification to triage the Homeless. You were a 'priority need' if you were classed as 'vulnerable', namely a child of 16 or under, disabled or pregnant; this put you on the list for accommodation. In other cases, the help was less forthcoming. You had to demonstrate, somehow, that you were more vulnerable than your homeless counterparts. That meant forms and evaluations – anathema to most homeless.

There was a reliance on charities like Hope Mission, the

soup kitchens, hostels and night shelters. They did more than all the state bureaucracy put together. The National Referral Mechanism, the Anti-Slavery Steering Group, the UK Housing Foundation– none of them made a meal, treated sores or produced a bed.

But all that being said, what did Shane *know* of homelessness? It was like knowing a country existed and that its people had a culture, without ever visiting. It was why Gracie had come up with the code, for herself and others who lived in the same land, and why there was still demand for Darren to peddle it for his purposes. She was the outsider here, in these four walls, the interloper into that private conversation. To the beggar or the tramp, she fell into the same category as the Spice leaflet.

'I'm Shane Ellis.'

The room had dispersed. She went to offer a hand, but his were in his pockets, and he made no move to change that.

'I'm a Deceased Affairs officer.'

'Yes. Karen told me.' Abrupt, bordering on rude. All the while the eyes moved, unwilling to settle.

Drawing out her mobile, she showed him the photo of the nameless. 'He passed away. I'm trying to establish his name, his background, any family. He was homeless.'

Darren put his hands on his hips. The lion writhed as the forearm muscle gathered. He shrugged. 'I don't know him.'

'You're sure?'

'Very.'

'He was close friends with a woman called Gracie. Did you know her? She wrote the code, the principles you use in your talks.'

'I knew Gracie.' There was a flicker in the eyes, some hint of emotion beneath the protective shell. 'I knew her from before the streets. We were in care together. Later I came back to Manchester. She showed me the code. Then I left. I only heard she'd died when I came back.'

'Did you know Gracie's full name?'

'There are no surnames on the Street.'

'You were in care with her.'

'It's the same there.'

'Did she ever mention family?'

'Family is what most of us run away from.' It was a vague hint about his own story; his speech had revealed nothing of how he'd come to be on the streets, or how long he'd spent on them.

'There was an older man she used to keep company with as well.'

'So?'

'Did you know him?'

He shook his head, but she felt – like a sixth sense – that he was lying.

'After she died, you began to give these talks, they're about the principles she'd established?'

'They weren't hers. I've adapted them. They belong to the Street. Not to any person.'

'Your talk encourages people to get off the Street.'

'And?'

'Do they? Get off the streets?'

'It depends. On whether they want to get off. I never did. Until it changed.'

'Why did it change?'

He shrugged.

'That simple, is it?'

'Why are you here?'

A threatening silence developed.

Coldly, Shane said, 'I thought Karen had told you.'

'Life on the streets is about *survival*. That's why I hold these sessions: so people don't have to learn the hard way. You people never understand that – that surviving, out there, on the Street, is all that matters. Creating a space for yourself. A way to live. There is no good luck, no bad luck, only what you make for yourself. And when you're dead, you're dead.' Now there was direct eye contact. Now he was glaring at her.

'I didn't—'

'No one saved this guy when he was alive. Whoever the poor fucker was. No one saved Gracie either. So why are you bothering now?' He pointed in her face, the previously calm exterior transformed. 'Your type, with your perfect upbringing, your stable job, your warm home, your idyllic family life... You don't know troubles.'

'I have my troubles.'

'You are *not* part of this. You have never been cold, never been hungry. We don't need your help.'

'Who is "we"?' She countered. 'You're not homeless anymore.' A glut of outrage welled up inside Shane. 'Does Hope Mission pay you for these sessions?'

'I'm fucking done with this.' He looked back as he left. 'Cunt.' The tattooed arm clattered a door against the wall on his way out.

Shane Ellis stayed in the meeting room for a while, replaying events, collecting her thoughts. It was a peculiar feeling to have sat there first, before anyone had arrived, only to sit there now after everyone had gone, as though matters had conspired to underline the transience of human interactions. She sensed a permanence, notwithstanding, at the heart of all that had gone on. Some kernel or essence. With a blinding clarity she realised it was someone who had not been present at all. That someone was Gracie.

The young woman abided in the mind of the enigma, Darren. She endured in the code she had crafted with a vagrant's eye. She persisted in those principles that helped the new, naive blood which settled daily along the canals, underpasses and backstreets of the metropolis. That was a legacy, no matter how short her turn on earth. It proved that inspiration might flower in the most miserable of circumstances.

And what of the dead young man? He was not memorialised.

Some figures faintly acknowledged the image of his frozen corpse, others denied knowing him. He had authored no code, left no legacy at all. Affinity for a young man she'd never met didn't make much sense, but it was exactly what Shane felt in that instant.

For he'd been in the room today, in the tentative frames of other ragged young men. The woes he'd shared with them had led to a common juncture, of choosing a hostile Street over an unhappy home. He was in her, because Shane knew herself to be an unknown rather than a Gracie, no more gifted in legacy than he. And above all he was in her miscarried child, the son or daughter who might have made 18 and entered the adult world, in the way he once had, before his name was ever forgotten.

BEGGAR

Two years earlier

It was unmistakably a human body, recognised in the instant as only a body could be. At first, he couldn't tell whether it was a boy or a girl, a man or a woman, for it lay flat to the ground, shrouded in clothes. Soon his eyes saw how the trainers were dirty and worn; the trousers were baggy; the coat, complete with hood, was discoloured in patches and holey at the wrists and sleeves. Red Milliner stood in shock.

Earlier that summer, the residents of Heaton Moor had noticed an alarming increase in beggars outside their convenience stores and rough sleepers beneath the overhanging front of the community cinema. About half of the residents were older, affluent types who feared for their well-being from such an influx; nearly half were middle-aged, liberal folk who feared for the well-being of the indigent poor. The result was a cancelling out of sentiments which could have been mistaken for apathy. Red's mother commented once that she would never give money to a beggar 'because it just encouraged addiction', and his father had swiftly agreed, but otherwise, it was a part of life which hadn't concerned the young man until now.

The corpse belonged to a homeless woman. He had been taking a shortcut through one of the back alleys that ran parallel to the high street when he'd seen the crumpled pile, half on the grey gravel and half in the scrub undergrowth. Her eyes were open. Her face was whiter than he'd ever seen skin before, as though it had taken on the colour of the underlying bone, except for the ripple of veins, blue and prominent at the temples, and a bruised cut underneath the left eye; long hair issued from the hood of the coat and was matted round her ears. Swollen fingers with gritty nails protruded from the cuffs.

Red had never seen a dead body before, but he didn't feel afraid. Death was often in his teenage thoughts, whether that be his death, or the death of others. It appeared, sometimes, as the ultimate escape from an unhappy life; at others, it spoke only of nothingness. From an early age, he'd been aware that it was coming, perhaps tomorrow, perhaps years away, but still, undeniably, coming; that it was something nobody talked about; and as with anything in his life, his parents were too busy to help him understand it.

Unlike his classmates, Red never had access to a phone, laptop or the internet, but the previous year he had discovered a book on human pathology in the biology section of the school library. He'd been astonished by its graphic imagery of stabbings, drownings, hangings and shootings; violent perimortem trauma; flesh decomposing following immersion; road accident mortalities; infanticide and the hallmarks of child abuse. He'd been even more surprised that it was on the shelf for any student to pick up. But then, why hide away that particular education? Kids of his age were taught about sex. Death, too, was a fact of life, only – he concluded – more taboo. It was why he'd smuggled the book out of the library rather than borrowing it on his card. Promising himself that he would return it at a later date, he'd stashed it at the bottom of his wardrobe like some exotic contraband.

So now he did a foolish thing. This was his chance to look Death in the eye, and in that split second, he took the opportunity. He crouched beside the homeless woman's body. He considered the physical form before him, the tiny details of demise and what it revealed to him. He saw the difference that always exists between a picture in the mind and the reality itself, stark and unadorned.

She wasn't asleep exactly. It was something else. Another state of being. The teenager moved closer and touched the open hand. The photos in the book were autopsies of the anonymous dead and inevitably dehumanising; in those clinical inquiries, there was a separation from the individual that had lived. But the homeless woman was still very much 'there', he thought. She was simply transformed. A recipient of the mortal touch. Red had the sudden, strange idea that Death might have a nature, and a style, that it imposed upon the living reliably, universally. That it might be an addition rather than a subtraction. And for that reason, Death didn't feel, at that moment, like an ending. It looked like continuity under a different guise and name.

Still foolish. To stand with a corpse rather than raise the alarm.

'Is she alright?'

A shadow, formed by the low morning sun, elongated ahead of the boy. He turned to find a resident of Heaton Moor staring at him, forehead gathered into a knot of concern. The man drew a mobile from his pocket and dialled 999 before Red could answer.

GUILTY

'Did you touch the body?'

'No.'

He lied out of fear.

'Not in any way?'

'No.'

'Why didn't you call us?' The police officer shifted in his seat as though he'd taken a personal affront.

'I don't have a phone.'

'Why didn't you knock on a neighbour's door?'

'I was going to.'

He'd been asked whether he would submit to a voluntary interview, but it was one of those instances where adults use words that mean the opposite, as there was nothing voluntary about it. It had begun gently, with a request for him to describe what had happened 'in as much time as he needed'; then tones had hardened, and questions sharpened. The police were not allowed to interview a 15-year-old, voluntarily or otherwise, without a responsible adult in attendance. They had waited hours for his mother to arrive and were on the verge of bringing in a social worker to address the requirement; finally, she'd appeared through the station entrance, a taut, impatient shape, his father a few paces behind as usual. Though she kept quiet throughout, Red could sense her burning unease, an urge to get out of the room, out of the building.

'Per eyewitness account, you stood over the body for some time – why?'

He wanted to ask how this eyewitness had seen him standing over the body 'for some time' and why they hadn't called the police sooner, but he knew that challenge would go down badly. Could he tell them the truth? That he'd stood over a dead homeless woman because he'd wanted to study a corpse? That he had a book at home full of dead bodies? No. These were things that he categorically could not say.

Red Milliner had been an unhappy boy from his earliest days, owing to one simple, ingrained truth: his parents didn't want him. Theirs was not a loveless marriage, as they plainly loved each other, but it was a loveless family, as they didn't love him. He didn't know why that was, just that it was as familiar to him as getting up in the morning and as unalterable as life ending one day, like it had for the Heaton Moor beggar. Out of desperation, he'd run away from home twice and returned each time to find that his mother and father had barely noticed he'd gone.

'Was she already deceased?' The police officer leaned in, eying him closely.

'Yes.'

His colleague picked up the questioning. 'Had you seen her alive previously?'

'No, I didn't know her.'

'Did you see anyone else at the scene?'

'Only the man who called 999. He arrived after me.'

'Was there anything on, beside or near the body that you removed?'

'No.'

'Did you touch her?'

That was the second time they'd asked the question.

'Red? Did you touch her sexually?'

The youngster shook his head vehemently. He swallowed again, not from guilt but from horror. His mother was staring at the floor. Surely they could tell by examining the body?

There is nothing worse for a child than silent treatment from a parent; it is as dark and unknowable as the pitch black that holds monsters. Red was no longer a child, but that particular fear had bred in him since the early years; it still exercised a power over him at 15 that he would have struggled to rationalise. He felt the terrible tumult in his stomach as his father drove home, obediently taking the wordless lead of his wife.

The police had finished their questions as abruptly as they'd started them. They'd left matters open-ended as to what further investigations they'd need to conduct and whether he'd get interviewed again, voluntarily or otherwise. There was an arrogance there, and he took note. They would keep you in suspense. They would communicate when they were good and ready. They would hang uncertainty over your future. He still felt the trust that comes with youth, and the trust born of innocence, that he couldn't be found guilty of anything as he'd committed no crime.

Ridiculous though it might sound, his parents didn't care whether he was guilty or not. All his mother would be worried about was the trades. As soon as they had come out of the station, she had tried to load the app on her phone, but it must have crashed repeatedly because she sat stiffly with the phone gripped, white-knuckled, through the ride home.

They pulled up in the car. She was stepping down before it had properly come to a stop. She had her keys out and was straight in the front door. Her husband was close behind her; Red dawdled on the driveway. He was overwhelmed with an awareness of his redundancy, his intense superfluity. If he disappeared in a puff of smoke, it literally would not matter.

The scene that greeted him when he entered was as bad as he'd expected.

'I've lost thousands,' she said, her voice a malevolent whisper.

His mother had started day trading through online platforms

about three years before. It ruled her waking moments and her every turn of mood. If she made a little money through an fx trade or two, then the evening would be calm, bordering on joyful, but if that fx trade went belly up, a night of sullen temper awaited. His father had learned to stand at the bear's shoulder, soothing, while Red took himself upstairs, out of harm's way.

It was what he did now. It was all his fault. The arrest. Her being away from her computer. It was like an irresolvable loop in his brain because some deep-lying sense told him that he didn't seek out trouble, that he hadn't wanted his mum to miss her trading opportunities… but he shouldn't have crouched beside the body. If he wasn't to blame, who was? It had to be him.

Red had realised that his childhood was abnormal from the age of five. He remembered the moment of realisation with great clarity. As usual, he was on his own in his bedroom and had been for several hours. Standing on the bed, he managed to pull himself onto the windowsill. Down on the street, he could see a family walking. There was a mother and father and a boy around his age, perhaps a little younger. The boy tripped, fell on his hands and burst into tears. The mother rushed to pick him up and comfort him. It was the warmth of her embrace which clutched Red's heart, the biting revelation that love, devotion and caring could all be made visible, that a child could experience them physically – and that he never had.

It was a more traditional form of gambling that had absorbed his mother in those years: the horses. The subject dominated his parents' conversation, peppering it with curious names and a flurry of numbers he later understood to be the bookies' odds. While he was banished to his room for hours on end with nothing to do except stare at the wall, they reviewed form books for jump and flat in a hive of concentration. Weeks would pass without a shower or bath until his hair was matted and his scalp itched. Sores in his groin meant they were forced to clean him with exasperation and haste. He was put to bed as early as possible and lay awake hearing the murmur of voices through the floorboards. There was rarely food in the house; as he grew older, he understood that it wasn't due to a lack of money, just that his parents were too preoccupied to head down to the shops. Everything was from a tin or packet; as soon as he was old enough, he had to prepare meals for himself. Often he cooked for them too.

For a long time, Red was convinced there was something wrong with him: that he was ugly or simply a bad child. Attempts to engage his parents, to seek or give affection, were rebuffed. Rare moments of attention left him hungry for more; it became a cruel, internalised seesaw of hope and loathing. Going to school and noticing how other kids' lives were different, he soon became an expert at concealing the nature of his home life. He was a good student, stayed out of trouble, made friends with his classmates and grew adept at reconstructing the family narrative. All to avoid others seeing the dysfunction and that he was to blame.

The first time he'd run away, he barely made it past the end of the street. With a tiny bag hugging his back, he'd retraced his steps and waited, watching the front door to his house at a distance. It did not open. That had burned deeply: he couldn't put into words how much he wanted his mother to come out with a frantic look on her face, desperate to find her son.

Red got off his bed. The house was quiet. His parents were counting their losses. Dusk had come; he felt his anguish increasing, even as the day diminished. He went to the window and peered into the dark. Rows of houses stood shoulder to shoulder far into the distance, each guarding a heart of light. He flattened his hand against the pane of glass as if communion were possible through touch alone.

How many families lived in those homes, he wondered. While children slept soundly on goose-down pillows, were there other young men as unhappy as him? Were there any out on the streets? Were they accused of things they hadn't done?

Through tears and with a terrible clarity, the young man apprehended his hopelessness and desperation. His solitude was absolute. No one would ever be on his side. Lost in the night, the world took on its true shape: inimical, purposed and hidden.

MELANIE

'Trampfucker' was what they had written on the board. They'd added 'Murderer' for good measure. He hadn't noticed anything as he'd come into the classroom with Dan and Joe; it was the head-turning and heavy glances of other pupils which had alerted him as he sat down. Mr Wilkinson came into the room and took a second or two to register the words.

It would always have been Mr Wilkinson's class where such a deed went down. He was a man who was afraid of the collective animal, who couldn't look it in the eye; his volume varied when he spoke; he swallowed if a student asked a question; he was continually rallying himself inside. And yet he wasn't some faded gent of another era, wearing an elbow-patched jacket and other day tastes. He was young, newly-wed, with a glistening ring on his finger. His hair was well-cut, and his clothes on point, but he simply could not meet the demands of the role.

Still, Red expected some reaction. No teacher could let someone write 'Trampfucker' on the board of his classroom without being seen to act! Surely it called for outrage, fierce questioning and the headmistress's immediate attention? Mr Wilkinson took a barely perceptible breath and wiped the board clean. The lesson began.

The young man was used to the adult world not protecting him and knew the only reliance of substance was a reliance on himself. But it was a sobering blow. He just sat there, voiceless. He hadn't touched the woman. What if people believed what was written? It was vile, evil.

As Red lowered his head to block out the stares and whispers, he noticed Melanie watching. Those dark eyes of hers had fastened on him from across the room. She had dark hair to match and something of the wild about her; he'd heard another student call her a gypsy, and the unannounced way that she'd arrived one day from another school, and an undisclosed place, further conferred upon her the status of a traveller.

He kept his head down for the rest of the lesson. Even Dan and Joe, on either side of him, said nothing. Then it was lunchtime, and they filed out.

'You alright?' Dan asked as they ate in a corner of the canteen.

'I'm fine,' he lied.

'Who do you think did it?' Joe looked at him through his round glasses.

'Dunno.'

'Did you recognise the handwriting?'

'Leave off, Joe,' said Dan.

'What's wrong?'

'Red would have said if he knew who done it.'

'Huh.' He considered. 'They can't have had much time.'

'Two words don't take much time.'

Dan scratched his chin. 'I bet other people saw them doing it. You should go to the headmistress.'

'It'll make things worse.'

'Or get your parents to.'

Red was silent.

'Whoever did it, when we find out, we'll sort them out for you!' Joe, full name Jeremiah, was about five-foot-two and couldn't have sorted out a 10-year-old. Dan would have stood more chance against an opponent. He was a sportsman and in most of the school teams.

In fact, Dan was pretty much the opposite of Red: sporty, popular and fancied by the girls. His mother worked for a catering company; his father was a builder. Everything seemed content and straightforward about his life. It was a wonder they'd ended up friends at all. A barrier remained between them, nonetheless, the one that Red had installed for the entire outside world. He'd never confided to Dan about his uncaring parents, the misery wrought by them, and the dream that he often had sat beside him in class, one of unmitigated escape.

'Can I sit here?' It was Melanie. She was alone, carrying her tray.

'I've finished,' said Dan.

'Me too,' said Joe.

They had never liked her and had told Red as much. They didn't like the way she tried to insert herself into their group. They hated how she'd homed in on their friend about five minutes after joining. If a boy and girl spent any time together, rumours started up like nobody's business, and that was precisely what had happened. They felt she'd done it to set tongues wagging.

His feelings towards her had been a constantly changing graph: early reserve followed by rapid familiarity; trust; distrust; and now an intimate caution. Her company was different to that of Dan or Joe: conversation deeper than a boy's, good or bad. She'd felt a connection for the same reason. She'd said he was unlike other classmates: older somehow, like he'd done twice the living.

He still wanted to trust her. Wanted to like her. She was pretty, and no other girl gave him the time of day. But each moment of attraction met its counter-moment of repulsion. He'd glimpsed kindness in her but also cruelty. She seemed vulnerable one day and in need of help; the next day, she was playing games; he could have sworn it.

'Who wrote that stuff?' she began. 'On the board.'

'I don't know. Certainly got people's attention.'

'No clue at all?'

'Nope.'

The girl dipped a chip in ketchup and ate it, considering.

In class, her look had been so fleeting, yet so deliberate.

Had she been involved? If she had, she wouldn't have been the one holding the pen. Hers would have been the invisible hand guiding the penholder, whoever that might be.

'I'm glad everything was okay,' she said, 'with the police.'

'Meaning?'

'Everyone's talking about it. They let you go. They don't do that if they think you did it.'

'Did what? I was never arrested.'

'Oh, weren't you? You still haven't told me what happened. Do you want one?' She pointed to the chips.

'There's nothing to say. I was walking to school. This tramp was lying on the ground. She was clearly dead. The police asked me some questions about it. End of.'

'Must have been awful, that. Just coming across her. What did she look like? Was it scary?'

'No,' he said truthfully. Less than two days had passed, but it already felt like a turning point in his life: one of the few times when he'd understood everything before him and experienced no fear at all.

'It is weird, though. I saw my grandma when she died. Died in her sleep.' She put the cutlery on her plate and pushed the tray to one side. 'I didn't want to see her, but my mother made me. She said it was what the family always did. She looked tiny, this tiny figure in a huge coffin. They'd brushed her hair and put on some jewellery. She wore this nice dress and a shawl. She was Hungarian, you see. The ceremony was in Hungarian.'

'What did you think of it?' he asked.

'It?'

'Sorry. Death, I mean.'

She laughed. 'What a strange question. I don't know. My grandmother looked a lot younger. Her skin was smooth. It was like she was a sculpture or something.' She paused. 'What did Dan say?' she asked. 'And Joe?'

'About what?'

'Death, what do you think?'

'Boys don't talk about death.'

'They're children.'

'They're my friends.'

'What am I?'

'You're Melanie. With your grandma,' he went on, 'when you saw her lying there, did it feel like the end? Like she'd gone?'

'I don't know. I mean, she *had* gone. Feelings had nothing to do with it. Why? What was it like when you saw this body?'

'Different,' he said, 'than I'd expected.'

'How?'

'I don't know,' he said impatiently, even though he did. He moved his tray to one side.

'Meaning, not the end? Red, talk to me. You can trust me.'

He averted his gaze. A lengthy silence followed. Melanie looked confused, and he felt a twinge of pity.

'Did I miss much while I was being interviewed for a crime I didn't do?'

'Boring maths, then boring English. Oh, and history. That was borrriing.'

'You bore easily.'

She nodded, smiling faintly. 'So, what did the cops ask?'

'Why are you *so* interested to know?'

'I'm not. But I wouldn't be a friend if I didn't ask.'

It sounded hollow to his ears. Was she a friend? His trust was at an all-time low. Joe had once called Melanie 'a control freak', and that label had struck a chord. The word 'Trampfucker' floated up as she watched him all the while.

'They asked me to say what had happened. That was all.'

There was an edge to the delivery of those last words, a finality he'd applied that stung her.

She stood up.

'Let's get back to class,' she said.

GRAVITY

When he came home that evening, his mother was beaming, which could mean only one thing: one of her positions had come in big.

His father was sitting in an armchair with a can of beer in hand, and his face was glowing. They talked animatedly together as Red let himself in through the back door.

'Here. Guess what your mother did!'

He didn't care. Someone had written terrible things about him on the classroom board for everyone to see. He was a joke, a laughing stock.

'I'll tell you exactly what I did,' his mother interrupted. In normal times she barely looked him in the eye. Now her gaze bore into him. 'I shorted the euro. And...' She raised a finger. 'I went long on the pound.'

'That's an understatement,' his father said. 'Long on the pound! Very, very long on the pound, more like.' They looked at each other and burst out laughing.

'How much did you make?'

'A pretty penny,' his mother replied. 'Let's just say that.' She was grinning like a Cheshire cat. 'I knew it would come in for me. And there'll be plenty more where that came from! I know *exactly* what to do now.'

'We're going out to celebrate,' his father said. 'You can have a takeaway.' He drew a five-pound note from his pocket and held it out. The young man took it.

His mother was looking at herself in the mirror, adjusting her hair.

'Love, get your Sunday best on. Let's go rip it up!'

Red knew the pattern well: the triumph, the largesse, the reversal of fortune that inevitably followed. At least their pleasure would be short-lived; for him, it served only to emphasise that he had never been the source of such unalloyed joy.

As they got ready for their night on the town, the young man took himself off to the high street, nominally to get a takeaway, but really to walk alone, away from them and the house. He passed by the alley where he had found the homeless woman, but he did not turn and look down it out of fear that someone might notice. The day after her death, there were fewer vagrants and rough sleepers to be seen, as though word had spread that the Heatons was an unlucky place to be a beggar. The cinema was open, and couples filed in arm-in-arm; the restaurants were filling up; families came out of the convenience stores with heavy bags of shopping, ready for an evening at home. On the wall that lined the main car park, he lay down right at the back where the trees and bushes were overgrown. There was a gap in the foliage, and above it, the sky, ashen, cloudless.

The last lesson of the school day had been about gravity. Lying on the wall now, staring up at that unvarying expanse, he felt as if he had no weight in his surroundings at all. He could rise up into the deep grey, up over the car park, the Heatons below getting smaller and smaller, the pub, the library, the glossy green park. He could rise until he vanished. Dan, Joe, Melanie: none of them would care. Not truly. His parents wouldn't even notice. He realised it was possible to pass through the world and leave no trace in the ether whatsoever, like a word being wiped from the classroom board.

A few days later, Red found something under the desk he usually sat at during geography. A metallic jangle gave it away as his foot made contact. The 'begging bowl' had coppers and a pair of tattered, fingerless gloves in it. A red marker pen had been used on the gloves to create 'bloody' patches. It was a new depth of pain and humiliation. He could have shouted and howled with anguish until the ceiling caved and buried everyone.

'Why are you ignoring me?'

'I'm not.'

'But you're not saying anything. It's the silent treatment. I know why,' Melanie said. 'You think I had something to do with the tramp stuff? The stuff under your desk. But I didn't have anything to do with it, I swear. I know who did.'

He held up his hand. 'It's okay. It's not something... I just. I don't want to know.'

'Is there someone else?' she asked suddenly.

'What?'

'Is there someone else?'

'Someone else than what?' He'd never been able to be rude to her. To tell her to do one. To buzz off and torture someone else.

'Oh, I don't understand why you won't talk to me about it. You don't want to share anything. Talk to me, Red. Why do you keep putting me on the outside?'

'There is no outside,' he said. 'Do you care about me?'

Her face brightened.

'Then let me the fuck be.'

She looked like she was about to cry. 'You... you...' She turned on her heels and left him standing in the corridor, looking a fool.

Another two days later, he got into a fight. It started when some lad had bumped into him; matters spiralled out of nothing; the lad shouted something unoriginal like 'at least I don't eat out dead fucking tramps'; the laugh that sprung to the lips of onlookers, including Melanie, had him punching and grappling on the instant. He would later tell himself that he'd been getting the better of the kid, forcing him to the ground first and registering blows to his ribs and jaw, when Dan intervened, hauling Red to his feet and dragging him away.

Joe had arrived too and leapt to his friend's defence. 'Come on then,' he snarled, 'if you think you're hard enough.' People laughed again.

'Fucking jew pussy,' the kid said, getting to his feet. Someone coughed loudly, a standard warning that a teacher was approaching, and the crowd dispersed. Once the adrenalin had subsided, Red found that he couldn't move his arm.

During the afternoon classes, he bore the ever-increasing pain. Sweat gathered at the base of his spine. He could feel the shirt tightening around his arm as it swelled. But he told no one. He would not let another indignity come to pass. He would not give them another thing to use. He was proud of himself when the school bell finally rang, and he could disappear, with even Dan and Joe suspecting nothing. 'See you tomorrow,' he said, managing to steady his voice.

UNUSED TO BREATHING

From the school to accident & emergency was a 20 minute walk. As he wasn't deemed an emergency, they kept him hanging around for two hours before they x-rayed the thing. Not broken, they concluded, just badly sprained.

At that point, he should have headed home, but he didn't want to go. The fight replayed in his mind constantly, and Melanie's laugh, impossibly vengeful, was among the images. Her true colours, perhaps. Or maybe a newfound spite.

He had never been to a hospital before, and his curiosity was piqued when he came across a site map in the atrium. One cluster of buildings was labelled 'Morgue'. He reflected that the homeless woman he'd found would have been brought there; perhaps she still occupied one of its cabinets, wrapped in her hospital shroud, waiting to be claimed.

It was an aspect of death that his book did not cover in any form: the non-medical content of its aftermath, how a body lay there refrigerated while arrangements were concluded for its disposal, the decision to bury or cremate. The casket, the ceremony, the send-off. The celebration of a life amid the mourners' grief.

He would never know the story of the homeless woman's life, how she'd come to die alone on the streets of Heaton Moor and whether anyone had grieved the loss. To be living on the streets, she'd possibly had parents who didn't give two shits, like his. His utter despair probably matched the one that had driven her. How had she made the decision, he wondered, to swap a roof over her head for an open sky.

The notion of escape – complete and binding – had never presented itself to Red in such a concrete form. To run away from home a third time, a final time. Not a protest or cry for help. No hope of his parents tracking him down, not even wanting them to do that. Moving on from that pain and the pain of school: a proper termination. He could visualise the preparation, the departure, the nights bedding down in the entranceways to tall buildings. There was freedom there, away from this prison, but there was also a fearful squalor.

After a while, he must have reached the far end of one wing of the hospital. Disappointingly there was no more road to travel. A large sign announced it as the maternity ward.

A man walked past Red and into the ward. Without further thought, the young man tailgated him through, keeping so close that they could have been visiting together. The man went into a room and closed the door. Red hovered in the corridor outside; any staff must have been on call as no one was around.

There was a window in the door, its curtain drawn back, and he peered through. On the bed lay a woman in a gown, and the man stood beside her. A nurse moved into view as she passed a small bundle to the mother. The father leaned in. Red glimpsed the baby's face, pinkly swaddled in the clothes, and a flash of open eyes, beautifully black. There was something inquisitive and naive in the gaze: a little animal-like, he thought.

The crying reached the young man's ears, muffled by the closed door; he watched the mother hushing, consoling. The electric light cast a stark gleam onto her hair and exhausted face. Once, his mother must have been through the same thing: a long pregnancy and a difficult birth. She must have held him in those first moments. What emotions, if any, had shown upon her face?

The door came slightly ajar. He could hear the smile in her

voice as the woman spoke. 'I'd like you to meet Arthur.'

The father took the baby in his arms like a box of fragile eggs and went to hand him back after a matter of moments, but the mother insisted, and he drew the tiny body closer, tucking in the fabric, looking down at the soft skin, the downy hair. 'Hello, Arthur,' he said. 'Welcome to the world.'

The dead, the books on autopsies, the process of shutdown and decay: here was the other end of the spectrum. Red had witnessed both within the space of a week.

Here was life commencing. It seemed shockingly tentative, so fraught with vulnerability – this new creature, unused to breathing, designed to rely upon another being, a thing of total need.

Some time ago, Red had decided that he would never marry. He would never have a child. He would never submit a child to the unhappiness that he endured. The reasons behind the unhappiness were not always clear because some days, he hated his parents, and on others, he loathed himself, but the conclusion was consistent: he would not repeat the misery. Lifelong solitude was the answer.

But this picture of domesticity shook him as if someone had grabbed him by the shoulders. There was a possibility of happiness here, in a setup like this: a triangle of harmony. There was order and goodness in the blankets neatly folded and draped on the back of a chair and in the cradle, which rested on a tabletop, ready for carrying the newborn home.

Could he find, somewhere, a world like this? He imagined himself being absorbed into it like a shell swallowed up by the wet sand on a beach.

The latch key scratched around the lock before it slid in. His arm protested as he turned it, and then the door opened. It was late and dark, but he felt elated. His whole body thrilled with the decision he had made.

The house was utterly quiet. His mother's laptop was shut; he could imagine the hours of work it had been put through before she'd retired to bed, gratified or sullen, market winner or stock loser. He'd been sure his parents wouldn't wait for him or wonder where on earth he was. Being right would have been a bitter victory if it hadn't reinforced his fierce intent.

He would run away a *third* time, a *final* time.

He would show them all. It would make them understand. He would make them sorry for the things they had done. His only regret was reserved for Dan and Joe, that he should leave them this way without a word of goodbye. But even for them, he couldn't go on.

Red's father kept a rucksack in the garage and an old sleeping bag as well. He packed the rucksack with some clothes, a towel and the sleeping bag. He took some money from his mother's purse. The theft gave him a surge of guilt, but he suppressed it; he wouldn't survive without any means at all. He always carried a cheap plastic wallet he'd found discarded in the street, and the money slipped neatly into its slot, behind his school library card. That made him think of his book on pathology secreted in the wardrobe; for a while, he debated things, given its weight and the practical vanity, but it felt wrong to leave it behind. Finally, he stored it at the bottom of his rucksack, then put the clothes and towel back on top.

The front door creaked open and closed quietly behind him. The empty street lay before him. As he took those first steps away from the house, he felt the fiery release of his freedom.

SHARKS AND WOLVES

Dawn had already broken when Red woke. He gripped the edges of the sleeping bag, lying inside it in the foetal position. He had caught the last bus into Manchester city centre. He was slumped in a shop doorway about halfway down Market Street, and his sprained arm ached terribly. A man was standing over him.

The police officer crouched as Red propped himself up in his sleeping bag. A griping churn started in his stomach as his mind was thrust back to the interview he'd been subjected to weeks before. If they learned that he'd run away from home, would that renew their suspicions? This could mean the end of his escape within 24 hours: frogmarched back to the Heatons in disgrace. If he had been bullied at school before, it was nothing compared to what lay in store.

'What's your name, son?'

He shook his head like a mute.

'How old are you?'

He shook his head again.

'Come on, lad. You can say how old you are.'

The young man pulled the sleeping bag tighter, up to his chin. He could see the heads of passersby turning to look at him: early bird Mancunians on their way to the office. He could see the disregard on their faces, not quite disapproval, and not yet disgust: a beggar accosted by the police was commonplace in the centre and no cause for concern unless things got ugly.

The man in uniform was matter of fact. 'Whether you tell me or not, I can see you're a young lad, and that puts you squarely in the bracket of being "vulnerable". Which means I need to take you to one of the shelters so they can take proper care of you. You won't last five minutes out here. I can tell from your gear that you're new to this game.'

Could he refuse? Not really. Red stood up, gathered his possessions and walked with him.

'How does someone your age end up on the Street?' The copper stared straight ahead. The inflection had made for a tired statement, not a question. 'You've been let down,' he said mysteriously. 'Take the help.'

He had brought him to a charity called Refuge House, and they waited patiently in a queue for the staff member at reception.

'Vulnerable,' was all the police officer said, guiding the young man forward by the arm. Then he vanished back onto his beat.

Red was equally against sharing his details with the charity workers. Being classed as 'vulnerable' might open doors for him, perhaps even secure some shelter, but getting deep into those processes might be another fast route home. So, he persisted with the obtuse head shakes and eyes-to-the-floor shoulder shrugs. But he hadn't reckoned on one thing: the smell of a cooked breakfast creeping down the corridor to the right of the front desk. As it turned out, there was a soup kitchen on the premises, with free breakfasts for rough sleepers; but the staff made things quite clear: you had to be registered with the centre, and you had to be off the drugs and the booze and generally not out to cause trouble.

The authorities always got you somehow, he decided; they always held some power over you. If he wanted the grub, then he would have to sign up. But for this, at least, the diligence seemed light. He made up a name, a date of birth and a former address. They assiduously wrote it all down. With frank ease, he vouched that he didn't have a drinking problem or some other soul-destroying addiction, that he wasn't given to antisocial behaviour, etc., etc. It all seemed to take an eternity while the aroma of hot bread and a sizzling fry-up tugged at his tongue, and his insides somersaulted with anticipation. He hadn't eaten since yesterday lunchtime. The cold doubled the famine. Nothing else mattered – the horrors of the night, the police, the future; the possibility of food captured his whole being. It was one of his first learnings in this new world. Never get yourself so hungry that you'll do anything to fill your gut.

The soup kitchen was warm and well-lit, with plastic tables and wooden folding chairs filling the central space. Before a row of shiny counters with shallow metal trays, a queue of vagrants waited politely for staff to scoop bacon, sausages, eggs, beans and more onto the round white plates held out to them. Most of the vagrants were men, but there were women too, and a range of ages, though few looked over 40. The smell of unwashed bodies hung noticeably in the air, a curdled note among the appetising ones.

Taking a plate and a tray, Red joined the line, and when his turn came, he asked for everything on offer. 'Thank you,' he said, unable to contain his gratitude to the woman who served him; he was almost shocked that a good meal should be so easily accessible to someone on the streets. If things were like this, it would be alright. He wouldn't starve. Did they serve other meals too, he wondered.

'Hello. Can I sit here?'

Red looked up from his plate. He had opted for the quietest table in the room, purposefully so, as he wanted to focus on his food and nothing else. A nervousness had come over him that a tramp might approach and want to interact; no matter how many times he reflected on his newfound homelessness, he couldn't visualise that first step of integration. The threshold between former life and prospective being was too pronounced and intimidating.

But it wasn't in him to be rude either. 'Yes. It's free.'

Only now did he notice how well-dressed the speaker was compared to others in the room. His jeans and sweatshirt showed no sign of dirt or wear, and he wore a chunky watch on his wrist. His hair was brushed, and he was clean-shaven. There was hardly any food on his plate, and he didn't even eat that, as if breakfast wasn't the reason for being there. A year or two older than himself, the young man had an accent which could be Polish. There'd been some Polish kids at Red's school, and they'd kept themselves to themselves, away from the rest of the class. Behind their backs, they were called 'the Poles', 'the Polaks', or 'Laks' for short.

'Thank you.' For the rest of his time on the streets, the youngster never heard anyone be so polite. 'You're homeless?'

'Yes.'

'You can work?'

It seemed an odd question. 'Work?'

'Yes. You want work?'

Red was silent.

'I work,' the Pole said. 'The money is good. I have place to sleep too.'

As he sat there hesitating, he noticed that a young woman had taken the seat opposite them.

'Is this your friend?' Red asked as much to change the subject as anything. He honestly didn't know whether he wanted work or not. The thought of a roof over his head, his own space and a sustainable way to finance an independent living appealed unquestionably, but what work was this? Backbreaking labour? It couldn't be that attractive, otherwise others would be pursuing it in droves. The Pole did not look at the young woman, just shook his head, which seemed a little odd, as though he already knew her but did not want to admit it.

Red examined the woman more closely. She could be Polish too, he supposed. She was fair-skinned, thin and had clothing which suggested she looked after herself just as well as the guy. Unusually, she was a redhead, her hair scraped back in a ponytail. Were there Polish people with red hair?

His voice had lowered. It was just above a whisper. 'The boss is very good. Very fair. We work on buildings. Good pay, sleep. The food is good too. Better than here. Then you have enough money – you can get your own place.'

'Do you have your own place?'

'Yes.'

Working on buildings... that could mean anything. 'How much is the pay?'

'You come, the boss can say. But don't worry. He pays well.'

Red could feel himself coming round. The funds he'd brought with him wouldn't last long. Although he felt pathetic for it, he knew he'd struggle with another night in the open, and each one that followed would be harder still. The disrupted sleep, the bite in your bones, the fear for safety... If there was a place indoors to sleep, with regular food, in exchange for some hard graft? He was young and strong enough. The Pole looked in decent shape; if he was prospering, surely Red could also.

'So, you want work?'

'No. He doesn't want no fuckin' work.' A third voice had joined the conversation and belonged to the red-headed woman. Hers was an unfriendly face, with brows which knit aggressively and a snarl for a mouth, but it was her voice which stood out most of all. It confirmed that she wasn't Polish. This was a native speaker. A Manc.

'Don't listen to her, friend. She trouble. Everybody knows.'

'Fuck off, Polish.' The young woman got to her feet. She was leaning across the table, limbs tensing, like she wanted a scrap. It didn't make sense. She didn't have the build to fight anyone, least of all the muscular lad who stood opposite.

He rose as well, but there was a languidness in his movement.

A decision had already been made that he wasn't about to get in any fight. The look he gave Red said: stay here with the woman and take your chances, or come with me, and you'll have work and a bed.

Trusting no one was one of Red's guiding principles, as no one in his life had proved themselves worth trusting, so now he faced a dilemma. Whichever choice he made meant trusting one of the two. But it is always easier to do nothing than to do something, and he remained in his seat. The young woman sat back down, and the Polish lad left without another word.

What followed was an incredibly long, awkward silence, so much so that he wondered if the woman would speak again. Having eaten half her breakfast, she tucked the remainder into a bread barm and pressed the top down. Finally, she grabbed a napkin from the end of the table, wrapped it round the barm and slipped the thing into her pocket. When she did speak, she eyed him fiercely. 'Keep away from them S&W. If you know wot's good for yer.'

Red gave her a blank look.

'The Sharks and Wolves.'

What on earth was she talking about?

A pause.

'I'm Gracie. Who are you?'

He swallowed. Everything was too much for him to take in, too odd, this new life with its strange characters and their inexplicable motivations; in that instant, he did wish, weakly, that he could go back to where he'd come from. Creep back into the house, pretend nothing had happened. Endure things again.

This was it, he realised. The true decision-point. Go back or plough ahead. This was the real moment of choice.

'My name is Red,' he replied.

ROOFS ARE FOR LOSERS

'Let's go,' the woman said.

'Go? Go where?'

'The Street. Where d'yer think?'

Red frowned. Following her lead, he took his tray and slotted it into one of the trolley racks. He put on his backpack. His stomach felt magnificently full, with the warmth of the food beginning to permeate his body.

Gracie brushed her way past other homeless who were lining up. She walked like a Gallagher brother, bouncing on her toes, hands out to the side like she'd lamp anyone who came too close.

The front desk was empty now, but there were leaflets about the services the charity provided, some stacked in plastic holders fixed to the wall, others pinned to a large cork noticeboard. His eyes skimmed the titles: if he were going to survive, he'd have to clue himself up on the resources that were available, like the breakfast he'd had.

'Wot are yer doin'?'

He turned. She was looking around, one hand on the door handle, and seemed generally agitated.

'I'm looking at these leaflets.' He held one up.

'Leaflets don't do fuck.'

'O-kay.'

Her eyes flashed. 'We need to go. We've just told Polish to do one, and he's gone off like a pissy girl. I don't think we wanna be here if 'e comes back with his capo. Do you?'

'What?'

'Christ's sake. Come on!'

Red felt like he would embrace the Polish guy if he came back through the door. He'd clearly made the wrong decision. This woman was the worst. She was rude and aggressive, and he struggled to understand half of what she said.

They turned left on exiting the charity; she cut down one alleyway, then another; she walked fast. The sudden narrowing of the scenery made his senses jump in alarm. Was he going to get mugged? Or worse? He thought of the small amount of money stashed in the plastic wallet at the bottom of his bag – all he had to survive on for who knew how long.

He balled his fists, ready to fight if he had to.

The alleys came to an end. They were back on one of the main roads. Gracie seemed to have calmed because her pace had slowed dramatically, and gradually he drew level with her, though they continued in a strange silence for some minutes.

The most natural question would have been 'Where are we going?' or even 'Who the hell are you?', but he held his tongue. There was no point confronting her. He would look for the right moment to escape.

'One of the first things to learn, 'ere, on the Street,' she said, 'is you have to keep movin'. They don't wanna bother with a moving target. Capeesh?'

'Who's they?'

'Anyone – the S&W. The Gimps. People who wanna 'ave a go at a homeless.'

'Gimps?'

'Pigs. The Dibble.'

'The police?'

Perhaps the girl was a petty thief. She was skinny, but she didn't look like a drug addict. It depended on what she might be using, of course; there were plenty of kids at school who'd been taking stuff and still turning up to class. She was clean looking but dressed boyishly; she moved with athletic ease; he could imagine her scaling a fence, breaking a window and running off before the authorities arrived. Wonderful to think that he was keeping company with a known criminal.

Only now did he notice a curious thing. She had no bag or possessions of any kind. People who lived on the Street didn't have much, but they didn't just curl up on the pavement, or if they did, they didn't last long. And if they had only the clothes they were standing in, they didn't look and smell like she did.

The look on his face must have communicated itself, or an act of telepathy had taken place because she said, 'B's looking after my stuff.'

He adjusted the bag on his back. He didn't ask who B was.

'Oh, I thought maybe you had a place to stay.'

'Roofs are for losers.'

He almost laughed. Shelter from the elements, some comfort and warmth, privacy, a basic level of safety – after last night that didn't sound like loser territory to him. Even the chance to store his rucksack somewhere appealed.

Most homeless had hiding places to stash their bags or possessions during the day, some corner of a disused mill or the undergrowth bordering a green space or, like Gracie, a comrade of the Street to leave them with, taking turns. It held you back if you were lugging things around, but if you didn't safeguard them, they'd get stolen or divided up in a matter of minutes. The Street had little sentiment for such naivety. At night, you kept your worldly possessions as close as possible, your bag a makeshift pillow held tight under your head.

But that particular street knowledge, and all the rest besides, was still to come for the young man called Red. And with it, an understanding of Gracie's ferocious resistance to being housed in any form. Why, in her words, 'roofs were for losers'.

BARTHOLOMEW

They had reached a canal, one of the many that crisscrossed the city, a defining keepsake of her industrial past. There were ducks to be seen, geese too, and the light shook over the surface as if nervous of the dark waters. Red had never seen a collection of water so desperately black; he could imagine it being the journey's end for many a drunk or accidental victim. Passing a sluice, against which flotsam nudged and jostled, he had a vision of human bodies drifting towards it, their wet, drowned heads bobbing against the gates. His book described what happened to a cadaver after days of immersion: the swelling, splitting, sloughing, the rise of gases and sickly odours, food for creatures of the water and the air. It stood in contrast to the neat serenity of the homeless woman's demise. A watery dismemberment. Such an ugly death, so disruptive of the human form. Could that still be the 'continuity' he'd glimpsed?

Nothing flesh-like surfaced as the young man and woman walked on, and they shortly came to a bridge. Under the bridge, whistling periodically in the shade, sat a man in a tattered, collapsible fishing chair.

'B!'

The first thing Red noticed was that the man who went by the name B didn't smell great. Gracie seemed oblivious; she went right up and laid a hand on his shoulder. She brought out the breakfast barm from her pocket. Red had thought she was keeping it for herself, but she passed it to the man. The napkin had stuck a little to the surface of the bread, and he peeled it back with grubby fingers. His face gleamed with appreciation.

He was an old man, clearly, though it was difficult to know exactly how old. A blue cloth cap sat on a head of grey hair, mostly white at the temples and where it matted behind his ears. The moustache and beard were whiter still, in fact, more white than grey; if the guy had carried any weight, the comparison with Father Christmas would have been inevitable; but there was no paunch, no ruddy port-enabled complexion; he looked rather like God, down on His luck. He didn't so much eat the barm as attack it, and the grease spread around his mouth. Balling the serviette, he scraped it away with clumsy pleasure.

Then he considered the youngster with a curious eye.

'Who is this fine-looking gentleman?'

Red didn't think he'd heard a posher, plummier voice in all his life. The words were crisp and articulate, the pitch a deep, cultured sound. It took him entirely aback, as if a frog had come out of the canal and spoken.

''E's called Red.'

'Red?' He polished off the barm with a final bite. Glancing up at the young man from his seated position, he squinted against the glare of the water. 'As in Red Adair?' He let out a booming laugh, and Gracie laughed as well, though she clearly understood the reference no more than Red. It was the first time he'd heard her laugh. It was carefree and genuine, and there was a certain music when their contrasting sounds combined.

'Yeah. I've 'eard some proper weird names, but this one takes the flippin' biscuit.' Gracie eyed Red with disapproval.

'Well, regardless, an absolute pleasure to meet you, sir. What brings you to the streets of this great metropolis?'

'I ran away from home.'

''E was at the soup kitchen. Doesn't know wot 'e's doin'. Shark almost had 'im. Jaws halfway up his leg when I stepped in.'

'Oh yes, and which villain was that?'

'Marek.'

'Best to stay away from those fellows, Red.'

'If yer don't wanna get egged or iced.'

The old man smiled a kind smile. 'My name is Bart. Short for Bartholomew.'

'And I call 'im B. That's even shorter.'

Red realised that he was still carrying his rucksack and eased it down from his shoulders, resting it against the wall that lined the underside of the bridge. There were other bags there, too; he pushed it up alongside them.

'Did you catch owt?' Gracie asked.

Bart shook his head, which was when Red noticed the strangest thing yet: that beside the chair, the man had some kind of improvised rod and a tattered old net.

'Sometimes the gods shine on us,' he replied. 'Sometimes not.' He paused. 'Time for a smoke.'

'And I'm goin' for a wander.'

Gracie snatched up the fishing net and sauntered off down the towpath.

The dirty fingers fastened around a pack of Rizla papers that Bart had dug from one pocket and a small tobacco pouch from the other. His legs became a table. In this operation, at least, the fingers were surprisingly quick and nimble.

'I used to play piano,' the man said, fluttering his fingers over the laid-out tobacco. He winked. Then he lifted the lot up to his mouth, licked the Rizla's edge and patted it down. Some tobacco poked out of one end like an overspilling bird's nest, but Bart didn't seem to care. Two flicks of a disposable lighter and it glowed, the earthy tang rising into the air.

'What job did Marek offer you?'

'He didn't say too much. Something about building work. And how his boss gave him a place to stay. How I could have one.'

'Hm. It's a rumour, of course, but they say Marek works for

Dudek, who heads up one of the Serbian families here. People think Marek is Polish, but he's not, he's a Serb. I know a little Serbian.'

'Serbian families?'

'The big crime syndicates. The Mancunian underworld. They're involved in all sorts of felonies.' He glanced around, and the young man couldn't tell whether he was being serious or just trying to scare the wits out of him. 'Arms smuggling, the drug trade, murder-for-hire. Cybercrime seems to be all the rage. And people trafficking, of course.' Bart let out a long, smoky breath. 'Doesn't matter where they get them from, they look wherever they can find, and it's a roaring trade. The offer of a roof over your head can be the roof of a prison.'

'How do you know Serbian?' Red asked, eager to change the subject.

'Oh, just on my travels,' he said. 'I travelled a lot when I was a young man. Saw beautiful Belgrade. The White City.' He smiled to himself.

The young man said, 'I've never been anywhere.'

'Now the legs are tired.' He rubbed a contemplative hand through his beard. 'When I was your age, I couldn't bear being at home in England. Not Manchester. I'm from the south. Have you heard of a place called Surrey?'

'I think so.'

'I was an only child, and it was incredibly tedious.' He snorted. 'And my parents were disciplinarians. Didn't allow TV. So I read books. Amazing what you can learn from a book, my friend. Do you read?'

Red shook his head. 'Not much. A little.' It didn't seem like the moment to bring up his book on dead bodies. 'I'm an only child too.'

'Are you?'

'My parents aren't strict. They just don't... didn't... you know.'

Bart's eyes were sharp, reading everything.

'"The voice of parents is the voice of gods, for to their children they are heaven's lieutenants." Shakespeare,' he said. 'Larkin said something similar, though not as politely.'

The young man smiled, unsure how to respond.

The old man had turned to look at the canal. His eyes followed the tiny undulations that disturbed the water's perfect film. 'I was just itching to go and explore all the places I'd read about. Nothing better than the real thing. So I did.'

'And were they better?' Red asked. 'Than in the books?'

There was this desperate impulse, deep inside his belly, to tell this stranger about his yearning for escape and what had brought him to this point, but he felt like he wouldn't survive the unpacking of those emotions.

'Different, my boy. Neither better nor worse. Merely different. The funny thing is that now when I have no home left, no place to stay at all, I want nothing more than to stop and rest here in this city.' Bart had smoked the roll-up as far down as it would go without burning his fingers, and he dropped it to the ground before grinding his foot on it. 'And what's your story, dear boy? Why have you run away from home?'

There was a shout, and as he looked up, Red saw that Gracie was coming their way, net raised in the air. She was beaming from ear to ear, and strands of ginger hair were plastered to her forehead with physical exertion.

'Look wot I caught,' the young woman said, setting down the net and pulling out one of the biggest fish Red had ever seen. It thrashed between her hands.

'That didn't take long,' Bart began, a begrudging admiration in his voice.

Red couldn't believe that such a creature had grown in the canals of Manchester.

'Wot can I say? Sometimes the gods shine on us. Or rather – on me!'

The bearded man summoned a bucket of water from somewhere and set the fish in it; the splash of the writhing animal echoed, loud and vibrant, against the arch of the bridge, way above their heads.

CHILD

In the context of overall council resources, the Deceased Affairs Department was a relatively small team of eight individuals covering the Greater Manchester area. Like many other departments, it was located in the Town Hall Extension, which sat between St Peter's Square and Lloyd Street. Shane got in at eight o'clock that morning while most of her colleagues were still commuting. She wanted to see what she could learn about Gracie.

Strictly speaking, the case she'd been assigned was that of the young man. Still, experience had taught her that 'breakthroughs' in identifying a nameless and in tracking down relatives often came tangentially. Despite appeals in the local press and social media, nothing had come up on him directly. She would take whatever lead she could get.

As a homeless that had overdosed, there was a high probability that Gracie, too, had been casework for a DAO, and even though she had died over a year ago, it did not take long for Shane to find her file with a First Name search of the database. It confirmed that one of her colleagues had indeed handled the matter after the pathologist had determined that the Spice was self-administered, and the police concluded that there was no foul play. She noted with interest that the colleague was Martin Bright.

His name had been freshly tacked to the office door. She knocked and went in. He was rattling away at his keyboard but smiled warmly and beckoned her to sit.

'How's it going?'

He looked around the room and nodded. 'Getting used to it. I suppose.'

'And Social Wellbeing?'

'It's strange to be working on the living as well as the dead.' He smiled again.

Martin and Shane had been peers for nine years before their previous boss left, and Martin had been moved into the seat last month. In moving up, he'd become a division manager for the council. He now looked after not only their group but also the Social Wellbeing Department, which worked on the agenda for public health, including substance abuse, suicide prevention and other initiatives focused on the unwell living.

'Do you have some time now?'

'Course. Always got time for you.'

'Posh coffee?'

'I live for posh coffee.'

They had been friends as well as peers before, and Shane was unsure how their interactions would operate now. In theory, a distancing needed to happen because the balance of power and authority had shifted in the relationship; but she wanted the pleasant things to remain. There were moments when the attempt to harmonise the two felt natural, and other times when it felt the opposite.

'How's the case?' They had settled into comfortable chairs in the Caffe Nero on the corner of St Peter's Square. 'It was a nameless just off the Gardens, no?'

'Corner of Oldham Street. That listed building.'

'Manchester's full of listed buildings.'

'The Yorkshire Building Society one.'

'Hm. Now that is a nice coffee.' He leaned back in his chair.

'The kid's thumb was missing.'

'Ouch.'

'From before he died, though. A while before.'

'Stopped him hitchhiking then.' He scoffed. 'Going to Hell for that one.'

'There was a young woman he used to hang around with. That's where I was looking to draw on your memory banks.'

'Fire away.'

'She was called Gracie. Died about a year before him. I found her on file; she was one of your cases.'

He stared out of the coffee shop window, eyes tracking the movement of pedestrians. 'I remember,' he said. 'Spice. Was an unusual one, that... Well, not the Spice, obviously... You know how I was a journo before I worked for the council?'

'Metro, wasn't it?'

'Manchester Evening News. There was a piece I worked on once. Death of a child. Can't remember the name now. But anyway, it was her sister. Gracie and... Lisa, that's it. Lisa. Terrible case of child abuse. The mother and her boyfriend got put away. It's one of those strange things. I recognised Gracie immediately. Soon as I saw the coroner's photo. She could only have been seven at the time of her sister's death, but it was a murder case that stuck with me. Our Beth was a similar age then.'

'What happened?'

'Well, the mother was a drug addict, the father always got her sorted. Doted on the children. But then he died of cancer, and a boyfriend came into the picture. That's when the abuse began. Pure evil, he was. Lisa was the one who got targeted, not Gracie, but of course, she witnessed it all. Ended up with the poor kid getting killed. Then there was the trial. The adults pleaded guilty and tried to make it on grounds of diminished responsibility. Didn't work.' He considered. 'Here, I'll phone up Peter, my old boss at the News. I did a feature on it. Not sure how helpful it will be. Would have been years before she met this guy you're looking into. But you never know.'

'Thanks.'

'Hate to say it, but it made my job easier. Recognising her like that. Gracie Knight, identification complete. Poor girl.' He scratched a cheek. 'Still, didn't get me someone to pay for the funeral – there was no family except the mother. Would have been a public health burial for sure.'

'Would have been? You mean it wasn't a PHB?'

'An anonymous benefactor came forward.'

'Sounds like something out of Dickens.'

'It happens. Not often. But it does happen.'

'Who?'

'Haven't a clue. Whoever it was, they approached the priest and the undertakers directly. They called me, said everything had been taken care of. Was Southern Cemetery, as I remember. And that was that. We were off the hook.'

ECTOPIC

It was a northern sky that lay over Manchester Southern Cemetery that morning. The one constant in this corner of the world was the changing face of the skies, and this one had changed for the third time in as many hours. Grey-bellied clouds spread as far as the eye could see, and the rain was tumbling down.

'I'm sorry,' the man said. 'I don't remember.'

As the cemetery sexton, his job was to tend the graveyard and its records. He was younger than she had expected, somewhere in his mid-20s she guessed. A particular social awkwardness radiated through his interactions; though keen to help, he often rubbed his head in frustrated embarrassment. Pale and thin, he could have been one of the ghosts whose life histories he administered.

'The benefactor bought the plot,' Shane went on. 'And paid for the service.'

'This was a year ago?'

'That's right.'

'And what was the name?'

'Gracie Knight.'

His finger inched down the entries in a leather-bound volume. The sexton's register, complete with hand-drawn maps of individual plots, was one of those rare instances of documentation resisting computerisation. Shane could hear the soft brush of the man's sleeve over the paper. Finally, the finger stopped. 'Here. We'd best take an umbrella,' he said. 'It's a bit of a walk.'

Eventually, they reached the plot. The gravestone still looked new. Rising straight and true from the cut grass, it had her name inscribed and the dates that she had lived. It was simple, but they were all the details that mattered. Shane had taken the chance to study the archive but saw no mention of the anonymous benefactor that Martin had described. When asked, the sexton had no memory of the arrangement either.

The DAO had brought flowers. She set them on the ground.

'Did you know her?' the sexton asked gently.

Shane realised as she turned to the man that he'd seen tears in her eyes. He wasn't to know that the tears weren't for Gracie. Neither were they for the young nameless. The sight of marked graves had got to her. She was thinking of smaller shapes, of little buds of life which did not reach fruition and had no token of remembrance.

It was a year ago that Shane had miscarried. Technically it had been an ectopic pregnancy. That was where the embryo implanted itself outside the womb – and that was pretty much that. A sharp ache in her stomach had been the sole sign. The doctors had informed her that the fertilised egg had not descended to the right place. Nothing could be done.

She still hadn't accepted the immediacy and hopelessness of the prognosis: unviable. While every disease of the living had some treatment, some way to halt, mitigate, or retard, this tiny being could not be helped precisely because of what it was: an ectopic. An ectopic 'by any other name' would still not... be.

'Not the best weather,' he mumbled, offering a tissue.

Shane looked again at Gracie's file. The photo was a headshot of her lying, like the nameless, on the pathologist's table. Her face was less emaciated and prematurely aged than his, and it was surrounded by a halo of red hair that shone vividly despite the stark treatment of a flashlight. It was a face that the nameless would have recognised in an instant, Shane thought. In the quiet of the graveyard, she took a moment to reflect on his grief.

Ryan had told her that some couples held funerals for their miscarried child. It was a possibility for their ectopic. 'Some kind of memorial, at least. It might help us.' She simply couldn't imagine it, though. There was no body. No identity. No memories at all. You couldn't commemorate such emptiness, could you? She didn't even know whether her ectopic should be considered as having been alive. Was it far enough along to count?

What Shane did know was that if her baby had implanted correctly, if nothing had gone wrong during the birth, and if there were no fatal infantile diseases, she would have a child now, over a year old. A boy or a girl. A Michael or a Sally. That logic was unassailable. There were 'ifs' there, but they were prosaic conditions in the context of modern medical care. They were prosaic enough for her to return to the thought obsessively and not move forward an inch.

If life could be so terribly painful, why were we all so desperate to live? She would keep imagining what might have been. Was it worth the torture simply to exist? On a day like this, under a cold, unkind sky, it didn't feel like it. But, like an old refrain, the thought came back: living was pain, but death was nothingness. Try as she might, she could not conceive of her own nothingness.

The grave in front of her, all the graves that she could see, were nothingness. Little abysses interrupting the smooth topography of the breathing world. Gracie was in oblivion. The lichen would gradually creep over the stones, a thousand rains would come and go, Nature would still teem, skirting round the nothingness, never constrained by the cessation of others.

'Public health burial,' the sexton spoke again, pointing to a distant gathering as they headed back the way they'd come. He rubbed his head, desperate for words to fill the silence. 'You know about those. In your job. Statutory duty. For local authorities...'

Shane could see the priest in his vestments, holding an umbrella in one hand as he made a consecration with the other.

There was a council representative at every such burial, and it was a duty she had carried out several times herself; it was just the two of them, plus the pallbearers, head to toe in black. There were no flowers or wreaths, no headstones, simply the hole in the ground.

Her ectopic had been liquified with injections of methotrexate over the course of several weeks before it passed out of her. It was a drug used in chemotherapy and had left her gasping with physical pain; each time they tested her blood, the hormone levels had indicated that she was still pregnant, and the rounds of treatment continued. The ectopic had clung on until the final bout. One of the hardest thoughts was that she had been complicit in the administration of the toxin, as opposed to the pregnancy failing naturally. She could never explain to the little thing why she'd had to do what she did.

She had never given it a gender, and she had never given it a name. In a cruel twist of irony, her ectopic was another of the Nameless, true identity unknown, like the young man who had lost his life on the streets of Manchester, and whose case she had been assigned to investigate. A variant on that tragic theme, for her nameless was never born, and its identity never got the chance to manifest; it was one of the vast lines which never materialised. And that's how her ectopic had remained for over a year: nameless; half thought, half person; an arrested future, a non-existent past.

There was no point in making a vow in such circumstances, any more than there'd been a point in laying flowers at Gracie's grave, but everything in that moment, from the unsympathetic rain to the pitiful, mourner-less funeral, compelled Shane to make one.

'Nameless,' she voiced silently, 'whoever you are. I swear to you. You will not have a public health burial.' She would solve the case. She would not let him go to ground without a name and a headstone to bear it. As she watched the priest turn away and the pallbearers begin to fill in the earth, a swell of inexplicable anger broke over her. 'I swear to you. On my life.'

The idiocy of it was not lost on her. A commitment was merely a commitment, nothing more. It did not mean she would succeed. You cannot will a name into existence.

PETRIFIED

As Shane returned to her car, there was a ping from her phone, and she saw that Martin had forwarded an email from his old boss at the MEN. Attached was the feature article he had described about the killing of Gracie's younger sister, Lisa Knight. In the quiet of the car, the DAO's eyes flicked over the screen, absorbing the tale of horror.

The article contained details of the post-mortem findings. In addition to a fatal head injury, there had been partially healed breaks of Lisa's ribs and old fractures of the lower arms and legs. There were flesh injuries and scarring consistent with restraint, recurrent beating, stamping to the stomach, biting and cutting. There had been intentional scalding, indicated by 'tidemarks' on Lisa's skin; cigarette burns to her limbs and more behind her ears; heated cutlery had been applied to her thighs. There was also bruising, laceration of the genitalia and other indicators of sexual abuse.

Shane lowered her phone. Gracie had carried the knowledge of her sister's tragic end and her powerlessness to stop it all those years – until her own last day.

There was a sharp knock on the car window. It was the sexton. He had a solicitous look on his face. He handed her a packet of tissues. 'I found a spare.'

'Thank you,' she replied. 'I'm quite alright now.'

He nodded, then glanced round uneasily, unsure what to say next. Shane felt a nudge of sympathy. It must be a pretty lonely job at times.

'That office of yours,' she said. 'Is there a kettle in there?'

'How did the young man die?'

'Exposure. He was homeless.'

'Where was he found?'

'The city centre.'

'I used to be homeless,' the sexton said to her astonishment. 'A couple of years ago.' The tea was poured into the cups, the pot set down again, the milk and sugar added, and the biscuit tin located.

'I wasn't very close to my family growing up. One night I messed up particularly bad and had literally no one left to turn to. It does hit you. Like, what am I going to do now? I don't know. I found some cardboard. Lay down somewhere. I managed to sleep that night.'

'Were you afraid?'

'Petrified. The thing is, though, it's not really about that first night. You'd be amazed how easy it is to fall into sleeping on the streets. And stay there.'

In all the years she'd been doing the job, Shane had never asked a homeless person why it was so difficult to break the cycle.

'For lots, there's an addiction that keeps them there, obviously. Could be the one that landed them there in the first place. Or one they've picked up.' He paused. 'No job equals no money. No money equals no place to live. But for most decent jobs, you need things before you even apply. They tend to be posted online, so you need internet access. A mobile phone so you can be contacted. A bank account for your salary. You need to be clean and smart.' He smiled weakly. 'You need to look like you haven't spent the night in an alley.'

'What about getting help? There are the housing associations.'

'Too many in need, not enough spaces. They can help you get work, but it depends what it is. I mean, there's no point getting into accommodation, and then you're trying to pay the rent on a zero-hour contract.'

There was something like anger in the sexton's voice. First impressions were famously misleading, and Shane saw that she'd been wrong about him. There was courage lurking in the slight frame, a strength beneath the gauche, tremulous manner. It spoke eloquently against the prejudices that formed a common social currency: that a rough sleeper's predicament was a product of their worth, that they were dumb, lazy, unemployable. They were not. They were merely in a different state of being, like they'd been driving down a motorway and crossed into the next lane, and now they couldn't cross back. Few would trust them, employ them, give them access to credit, all the things that the lives of the Homed were built upon. From your position, you glanced across with a shudder of gratitude that it wasn't you in the wrong lane without realising that only a dotted line lay in-between.

'You're not on the streets anymore.'

'No. The church was running an outreach scheme. I wasn't sure at first. I don't believe in God for a start.'

Shane smiled.

'It turned out okay. Don't get me wrong; I'm not saying this is the answer to homelessness.' He laughed, the self-conscious rub of the head returning. 'It's not exactly a job most people would want. Looking after a graveyard.'

'Do you have accommodation now?'

'Yeah. Not a mansion. But it's got four walls and a roof.' A minute or two passed. Then he turned and said: 'What truly saved me, of course, was the Beggar's Code.'

Shane nearly knocked her tea over.

THE CODE

'You know the Beggar's Code?' She explained how Karen from Hope Mission had shared a copy with her. That Gracie was its author.

'I'd just arrived on the streets,' he said. 'There were copies of it at the first shelter I went to. A young woman came and talked about it.'

'That was Gracie.'

'I hadn't realised,' he said.

'What was she like?'

'Nervous – I remember how her hands shook. Clearly smart. Sharp as a tack. A Mancunian,' he said and smiled.

'Was there a young man with her?' She hadn't shown him the photo of the Nameless yet. She did so now. 'Do you recognise him? From the talk, or just generally – you must have been homeless at the same time.'

'No.'

'You said the code saved you. How?'

'Bit difficult to explain, really.' He was thinking. 'It was something to hold onto. There's a pride there, in the words. Do you know what I mean? Everything else is basically telling you you're a piece of garbage, that you're failing at everything. The volunteers at the charities do their best, but who wants to be defined by charity? The code says that you still have principles to live by. That you're worth something. That there can be honour in homelessness. At least, that's how I felt. Does that sound ridiculous?'

'No. It doesn't.'

'I wouldn't have got through those first months without it being there, in my pocket. Even though, ultimately, I did move on from it. I did leave the Street.'

'Do you ever miss it? The Street?'

'Bits, sometimes. But no. Overall, it's a horrible place.'

'There are pieces of the code that I don't understand.' She brought out her phone. 'Can you explain them to me?'

'If it would help.' He read from the screen.

> '"To you who have no home
> No room to call your own
> To you who walk the streets
> And have no bed in which to sleep
> To you who left the strife
> Of that sorry other life
> To you who have no clue
> On how or what to do
> We offer up this humble code
> For getting by on the beggar's road."'

'That was me,' he said, looking Shane in the eye. 'I had no clue what to do. No clue at all.' He cleared his throat. '"One: never bum from a bum."' He nodded. 'Basically, it's okay to be a bum. You ask for charity from the rest of the world. But you never beg from each other.'

'Why?'

He considered. 'It's degrading. Plus, it's upsetting the natural order – the homeless person begs, the muggle gives.'

'What's a muggle?'

'It's from Harry Potter. A non-magic person. Anyone who isn't homeless. You and I are muggles.' A grin.

'"Two: beggars can't be choosers." You've no idea what each day will bring: whether you will be hungry or full, whether you will be sick or well. You take what comes and make use of it however you can. It's a mindset thing.'

'I get it.'

'"Three: God bless the muggles." A muggle is not a bum, and a bum is not a muggle: their lives differ fundamentally. But the muggles are to be treated with respect. They give the Homeless everything they have.

'"Four: clean kids are mean kids." I know that sounds like 'clean' in a drugs sense, but that isn't what it means here. It means personal hygiene. It is vital – for your health, your self-respect and the respect of others.'

'And how do you do that?'

'Washing facilities at the shelters. For clothes. Showers too. Some people tailgate members into gyms or swimming pools. Nice bit of unintended charity there.' He smiled.

'"Five: there is safety in numbers." The streets are dangerous. Find out who you can trust. Do not spend those nights alone.

'"Six: eat or be worm's meat." It's the most obvious rule you could ever come up with, but it's also the most neglected. I remember being hungry constantly for the first week. Then your stomach shrinks, food doesn't come along regularly, and you forget how important it is. Drink and drugs replace proper food.

'"Seven: a newspaper is an insulator." I'd group this with "Eight: layers are saviours." and "Nine: give use to the useless." It's so hard to keep warm. Newspapers, bits of old cardboard, plastic sheeting, whatever comes your way is useful, particularly in the wintertime. The city's full of discarded rubbish. You'd be surprised how you can mend and make stuff.'

'I would be very surprised,' said Shane. 'Seriously, I wouldn't last a day.'

'"Ten: a shark is a wolf is a shark."' He looked serious. 'There's a queue of people right round the block looking to take advantage of you. They know you're hungry, cold, wanting work, a bed for the night. They pose as people who want to help. But they're sharks; they're wolves, all of them. And it's up to you to see them for what they are. There's a whole underworld of human trafficking, prostitution, slave labour. Getting made to work on farms, building sites, nail bars, car washes, the backs of restaurants, even in private homes. Particularly for immigrants. They take away your passport, force you into cannabis cultivation, theft, counterfeit goods.

'"Eleven: trust not the Gimps." The Gimps are the Greater Manchester Police.' He sighed. 'I hate to say it, but she was right on that. I can't tell you the number of times I got moved on or spent a night in a cell when I'd done nothing wrong. They showed no interest in crimes against the Homeless. We were always seen as the source of trouble, never the victim. They took the side of a muggle in any situation.

'And finally, "Twelve: shelter from life." If you're on the streets, you've probably escaped your old life because it was bad for you. Domestic violence, debt, whatever it was. The Street is your absent mother, the friend you never had; she'll shelter you from that previous hell. That's the most important message in the code.' A pause. 'But it's also the piece I turned away from in the end. I realised the Street isn't a shelter. She's the opposite.' The sexton looked at Shane again, and his gaze showed a glassy resentment. 'She's a prison. I wanted normal things again. Strange as it may sound, living on the streets can become an addiction. You have to want to get off them. Want it badly. You have to tackle what's in you – if you can.'

'Whoever gave you this role must have seen that in you,' Shane said. 'Your potential.'

He bent his head in humility.

Then: 'It could easily have been me.'

It took a moment for her to understand what he meant and a moment more to grasp why he had confided so much to her.

A Deceased Affairs officer appreciated the narrowness of that other dotted line, the one that existed between life and death.

'It could easily have been me in an early grave. Instead – now I look after them.'

REDUNDANT

'Was the article useful?'

Martin had poked his head out of his office as Shane walked past.

'Pretty messed up life, the girl had.'

'Do you have a minute?'

'Sure.'

'I had my first catch-up with Alan yesterday.' He gave a look. 'Wants the team downsizing. By two.'

'Wow.'

'Don't tell the rest.'

'My lips are sealed.'

'General cuts across departments, we're not being singled out.' He tapped a pen on paper.

'He doesn't waste much time. Am I one of the two?'

'No, you'd be the last to go. You know that. If you were in my shoes, who would you be looking at?'

'I'm not in your shoes,' she said, though not unkindly.

'But if you were.'

'Well. Denise is close to retirement. And it's no secret that James has been looking for other roles. You could approach them.'

He nodded. 'Feels like a test. From Alan.'

'Perhaps, but you're up to it.'

A glance at his notepad. 'He had reports on us, our performance over the last six months. Said we take too long to close cases.' He read out a slew of metrics: 'Caseload per staff member, Average time to close, percentage of Nameless identified, monthly cost of PHBs...'

'Easy for him to say. He isn't doing the investigating.'

'We'll need to tighten up.'

'None of this was mentioned to Rob when he was in charge.'

'Unless Rob sensed it was coming?'

'He would have said.' Shane paused, watching Martin. 'You should let the team know so everyone is clear on what's expected.'

Day three of her investigation had come to an end, and she was still no closer to identifying the young man who'd died of exposure on the corner of Oldham Street. Martin's comments on metrics heightened the pressure she already felt to turn the Nameless into the Named. In her stomach sat the gripe of time running out, of her promise at the cemetery slipping beyond reach.

Was it so important to have a name, really?

The whole of the animal kingdom got on very well without them. Only humans felt this desperate need to label, classify and individualise. A rabbit did not know the nomenclature of a falcon. All that mattered were the sharp claws and beak and the breakneck diving speed that marked it out from others, bringing death. Named or not, it was a predator, and the rabbit was prey, and there was a natural order to that arrangement, embedded in design and instinct, that didn't beg for words to give meaning.

But perhaps that was the natural order for humanity: to be 'the labelling animal'. Language wasn't possible without the means of reference; our activities could not take shape without some way of dedicating attention to individual objects. The name itself didn't matter, merely that there was one: 'a rose by any other name would smell as sweet'. Dedicating attention to an object. It sounded so pragmatic and short-lived. Attention lasted as long as it was needed. Didn't that mean, then, that attention was wasted on the dead?

If it was so pointless, then she, Shane Ellis, was also redundant. Why was she giving all her attention to a young man, full name unknown, when he couldn't witness it? What was the point of 'dignity'? Funerals, ceremonies, rituals?

Sat at her desk, wondering what step to take next, it felt like a losing battle, where the prize itself remained unclear. Was she doing this job just because it made her feel better? Had it become an addiction? She didn't know.

Some people were born without the love and attention they deserved. That wasn't her battle. They died alone – label lost – and there was nothing you could do about how their life had been. You couldn't restore its meaning in death. Shane shifted uncomfortably in her seat. Huge numbers of people never even got born. They never made it through the gates of life at all.

The DAO shut down her PC for the night, said goodnight to the others, and took her coat from the stand by the door. As she left the council offices, she noticed a boy of about five or six standing on the steps of the Albert Memorial. His tiny body was swallowed up by the canopied monument, its statue of Queen Victoria's consort stretching far into the dusky sky above. He shifted from foot to foot, glancing about and fidgeting.

'Have you lost your mummy?'

The child nodded.

'Don't worry. I'll stay with you until she comes back.'

A steady stream of muggles went by with the brisk stride of being homeward bound, their eyes heading for the trams or, further afield, for the trains at Piccadilly Station.

'What's your name?'

'Charlie.'

Charlie was suddenly close to tears. 'She's not coming back, is she?'

'Oh, I'm sure she is.'

Shane bent and patted the back of the boy's head. The hair was soft, and the palm of her hand absorbed its gentle warmth. He looked up at her, his gaze searching for reassurance and human connection. She held his hand.

'It's my fault,' he said. 'I wanted to look at the statue.'

'I can understand that. It's a pretty impressive statue.'

'She'll be angry.'

'I'm sure she won't.'

'Mummy will be angry.'

'Don't worry. I'll explain to her.'

'Charlie! There you are!'

'Mummy!' There was an embrace over the exchange of names: an answer, if any, as to why they mattered. Shane was not called upon to explain, and she watched as they melted into the bright lights of Cross Street.

'Goodnight, Shane,' a voice called out behind her. It was Martin. His sound echoed across the square. She turned to see that he was leaving the office too, heading in the direction of Deansgate, coat collar turned up. Moving quickly, he slipped into the muggle herd and was gone.

In the coming cold, Shane thought quietly of mothers and children, of metrics and measurements. She thought of fertilised eggs getting lost on their way and how a few centimetres could mean everything. The whole of life and death in the span of a boy's hand.

REPOSITORY

The building was on the outskirts of Manchester, in an area called Openshaw. From the outside, it looked like a library, a squat brown-brick structure with glass windows and hints of quiet activity going on inside; but Shane knew that the most interesting thing about the place was what took place below ground. It had the Greater Manchester Police insignia by the door and RIAE printed in block capitals. A sign at the front desk elucidated: The Repository for Investigative Artefacts and Evidence.

There were statutory requirements around the retention of evidence sourced from crime scenes or generally obtained during police investigations, and this was one of the main storehouses for such material. Security was tight, though the most sensitive artefacts – for example, those featured in prosecution cases – were held elsewhere. She had phoned ahead and scheduled an appointment, as all visitors had to be accompanied. It had taken a couple of days for confirmation to arrive.

Having signed in as a visitor and clipped the badge to her lapel, Shane sat in a chair by the entrance and waited. The odd person wandered past, lanyards and passes around their necks, hands empty for the most part, except for one carrying a cardboard box.

A man approached after 10 minutes. They shook hands and headed to the lift. He had a stooped back and didn't look in the strongest health, but he talked with the officialese lexicon and inflections which marked him out as a career policeman. RIAE was where coppers went when they were too young to retire but too old to be chasing crooks.

The man was incredibly talkative. On the way down, she heard all about the recent reordering of the repository, its dedicated temperature and moisture control system, plans for creating three further sites in the north of England, and how he felt protocol could be improved. Apparently, he had personally presented those ideas to the assistant chief constable and sensed it was only a matter of time before their adoption.

'Is this your first visit to our repository?'

The lift doors opened on level -3. They stepped out into the subterranean floor, its white shelving packed with plastic boxes and crates stretching as far as the eye could see.

'No, I've been a couple of times before.'

He looked a little put out at the missed opportunity to weigh in with further information.

'It was a while ago, though,' she said encouragingly. 'Things could have changed. Especially if there has been a reordering.'

His eyes lit up.

'Were you provided with a list of visitor rules on arrival?'

Shane looked blank.

'Typical! Those jobsworths on the front desk!' He snorted. To the left of the lift was a seating area with solid-looking tables. It was where boxes were brought for examination. The lighting was particularly stark. He indicated for her to sit. 'Well, no harm done. I can walk you through verbally.'

Twenty minutes later, Shane's companion was comfortable that he'd put the world to rights and trundled off to retrieve the box she'd requested. He had given her disposable gloves; she slipped them on as she waited. After a minute or two, she rose and wandered away from the area. The floor-to-ceiling shelves towered above her. She was alone, and it was eerie. Only the sound of her feet treading over the soft carpet tiles broke the underworld silence.

This was the section of RIAE dedicated to her trade: the John Does and the Jane Does. The possessions found beside an unidentified body – the mundane or the treasured, the everyday or the keepsake – wanted administration as much as the corpse itself. If an identity surfaced and relatives materialised, the belongings passed to them directly, sad inheritance from the figure they'd once known; otherwise, their home was here, boxed and shelved with the rest of their kind.

It was a poignant sight, the racks upon racks of containers, like so many bottled souls, stretching away from her to the limits of her vision. All those rich, individual lives: here were the signs that they had existed, tokens of fact if not remembrance; here too was the tally of failure, for each box was a failure by the authorities to rescue these beings from blank, mortal anonymity.

For every label that was absent in the real world, the repository generated a new one. Container reference 001-2784-2 was a name, too, of sorts. Beneath printed tags, the crates obediently held their contents, which had been neatly bagged for preservation's sake. Again, Shane Ellis was struck by this peculiar facet of humankind: the obsessive order, the cataloguing, the fruitless diligence and care. Every year a batch got incinerated when the retention requirements elapsed. The reference numbers were consumed by the fires too. It was the final acceptance that the unknown would never be known.

Soon enough, the articles that had been found on the young nameless would make their way here. Time would tell whether it became their permanent home and last stop to oblivion.

'Sincere apologies for the delay,' a voice travelled down the floor. The man reappeared carrying a box.

'Not to worry.'

He resumed his formal way of speaking. 'I retrieve all materials from their shelf location prior to visits and stow them in a room designated for that purpose. A colleague must have shifted it in the interim. It had been relocated behind a door, would you believe.'

They returned to the space with tables and chairs. He slid Gracie's box onto it. Although she was not a Jane Doe, her box was still stored at the repository as there was no family member to take ownership of the possessions: her father and sister were dead, and her mother was in jail. The lid slid up and off.

Protocol required that the man be present while Shane went through the possessions, but he seemed to appreciate that her time for quiet concentration had arrived; he set himself at a remove, hands upon the back of a chair, letting the DAO do what she needed to do. She was grateful for the space.

Inside the container was a rucksack. She lifted it out, unfastened the clasp and looked inside. She removed the items one by one.

Hallmarks of the code could be seen throughout in the transparent order and attention to self-care. Her clothes were laundered and folded: two sweaters, a pair of trousers, t-shirts, gloves (which looked like they'd been repaired a couple of times), underwear, socks and a wool beanie. All were in good condition. There were the tools for personal hygiene, just as there had been in the possessions of the nameless: a toiletries bag with a toothbrush, toothpaste and soap; it contained wipes, a comb and brush, hairpins and some makeup. There were sanitary towels in the side pocket and in another a shallow tin with hoarded contents: rubber bands, pins, needles, thread and a few other bits and pieces. Shane was instantly reminded of the ninth tenet: 'give use to the useless.'

At the bottom of the rucksack was a cheap fabric wallet. It was blue and opened and closed with a velcro strip. Shane instinctively felt that it wasn't Gracie's, but one which she'd somehow acquired and adapted to her purpose. Inside the main pocket were two photos, carefully folded to fit.

The young woman herself was in the first one. Seeing her alive gave Shane a sudden jolt. The red hair was unmistakable, and she had been snapped mid-laugh and in profile, head thrown back and eyes shining. The backdrop to the photo was one of Manchester's waterways, with a lock just visible. A tall building rose in one corner, mostly out of frame; it looked like an old cotton warehouse, heavily weathered across its red-brick facade and shadowy dark at the windows. Many such buildings had been torn down in recent years as part of the city's burgeoning regeneration, but some had survived the cull, like the older oaks in a forest, taking their chances with the attritional elements or undergoing conversion as fashionable apartment complexes. Although the DAO could not place the scene exactly, she would have put money on it being either Northern Quarter or neighbouring Ancoats, where the remnants of history had a particular foothold.

There was an elderly man in the photo. He had a huge white beard, the kind which would have given Father Christmas or God, for that matter, a run for their money. His eyes were twinkling at some joke lost to time. Perhaps he was out there still, on the streets of Manchester somewhere, if only she could find him.

The second photograph was somewhat older. The woman must have looked after it carefully for a number of years. No need to puzzle over the identity of the four subjects in the shot: Gracie, her sister Lisa, the mother and the father. The family resemblance was plain to see. Gracie looked five or six, Lisa about three – and there were hints of it being a happier time. The older girl had her arm round the younger girl. They squinted against the summer sun and smiled in blithe delight. Sisterly love spoke in the way they stood: the stance of playmates, fierce companions, thick as thieves. One would soon become a victim, the other a survivor, a distinction drawn simply by the wickedness of others.

Shane's eyes gravitated towards the mother. Of the group, she alone remained in this world, incarcerated for a horrific crime against her child.

Could you read evil in a face? No, Shane didn't believe so. Wishful thinking to glimpse it in the eyes of humanity's worst; it was merely hindsight's imprint. Nothing of the mother's dark heart or cruel propensities were previewed in her features. There were, perhaps, the signs of drug addiction: something worn and puffy around the eyes – an ageing before her time. Shane could also detect a fraying of the relationship between the two adults in the distance that they stood apart. The man was tall with brown hair. Otherwise, he was rather nondescript. Strange to think that he had been the hero in that dysfunctional setting before Fate had come and shaken its pack of cards.

There was something in Nature, Shane thought, about the relationship between fathers and daughters, just as there was between mothers and sons. She thought of her own family. There had been a depth to the relationship with her father when he was alive that wasn't there with her mother. A closeness that transcended.

Gracie had made use of the wallet cardholder as well. There were two additional items stored there. The protruding edge of the first caught her eye, shining under the overhead light. It was bright red with gold filigree and flourishes, and as she teased it out, Shane instantly recognised it for what it was.

On her phone, she pulled up the picture of the torn card found on the body of the nameless. This was its sibling. Conclusive proof of what the young man and woman had meant to each other. She brought together the real and virtual halves of the bookmark and read the completed quotation:

'What's in a name? That which we call a rose by any other name would smell as sweet.'

Slowly, reluctantly, the Deceased Affairs officer moved them apart again. Such separation resonated desperately within her in ways she couldn't have explained. Gracie and the nameless had never known her, and she had never known them; it was a memento ripped in two, nothing more; they were both dead, yet it seemed to matter terribly.

Her heart leapt as she slid out the second item, also a piece of card. In the corner of her eye, she saw the old police officer stir as though recognising from his investigative days the thrill of a breakthrough. It was a school library ticket.

No name of the school on it, nor a borrower's name, but there was a borrower number, written in bold and in biro: 334. It was another reference like those in the repository, another label from an alternative schema, except this one, perhaps, conserved the link to a glorious, original name.

POTATO

Without some biblical magic, a fish split three ways does not go very far. While Bartholomew was left to kill and cook the thing, Gracie and Red headed in the direction of Piccadilly Gardens and further sustenance. The young man was not terribly hungry after the large breakfast he'd had, but he would quickly learn that anticipating and acquiring your next meal, like some urban hunter-gatherer, was nine-tenths of the day's activities when you lived on the Street.

'The Muggles will be out,' she said, setting off briskly.

It was a routine with which he would become very familiar: at roughly 12 o'clock, carrying through until at least one-thirty, the working folk of central Manchester poured out of office buildings to take their lunch breaks, shop and generally take in the air. With them came not only the joys and frustrations of their morning but also the money in their wallets and a healthy guilt at walking past homeless people while tucking into a sandwich.

Red stopped dead in his tracks.

'I'm not begging,' he said.

'You wot?'

'I said I'm not begging.'

Abject visions of himself, sitting cross-legged on the city's street corners, assailed his mind: the outstretched hands, the humbled glance, the pleading gratitude, all while the 'muggles' looked on, perhaps muggles he knew... maybe even his classmates. It didn't matter that they shouldn't be in town at lunchtime on a weekday. Only that they could be there... bunking off, excused leave, whatever... He felt sick to his stomach. What if Joe saw him? Dan? Melanie? Every fibre of his being said no, like a horse backing down from a fence. 'I can't do it.'

'Beggars can't be choosers.'

Her face was right up close to his. He had never got a good look at her eyes before. The colour was the most unusual he had ever seen: not ginger exactly, warmer perhaps – an amber shade – the eyes that a tiger might have as it watches from captivity. He could see a caged anger lurking, and it was about to come out.

'And 'ow the fuck you gunna last on the Street?'

'There's the soup kitchen.'

'That went well, didn't it? Nearly got trafficked over breakfast!' Her voice tightened. 'Yer can't get three meals a day from the 'andouts. And yer can't get no dough from 'em neither.'

Red went to mention the fish but thought better of it. He also thought of the small cache of money at the bottom of his bag, but he wouldn't be mentioning that either.

'Don't think of it as beggin'. Call it wot yer want. Charity. Alms for the blinkin' poor. Call it wot yer want, mate; I don't care. But you'd better had do it. Get yer shit together pronto, or yer might as well get yerself back home to mum and dad!'

His fury came out of nowhere. 'Fuck off!'

'No, you fuck off!' Suddenly she had hold of his collar and was trying to pull him down into a headlock.

'Ow! Get the... get off!' He broke free.

She turned on her heels.

He kept himself at a distance, unwilling to walk alongside her, a maelstrom of thoughts in his head. He wasn't going to beg, and that was that! No way was he changing his mind. Over his dead body! He would find other ways to survive! He would prove her wrong. Did she think it was easy living at home all these years with the parents he had? Did she think he wasn't resourceful? He would show her. Who the hell did she think she was anyway?

They'd met that morning. Who was she to be ordering him around? Shouting at him in the street, that glare in her eyes – right at him? He had a good mind to walk away there and then.

He was still seething when they reached Piccadilly Gardens. Gracie gave him one last contemptuous glare and nod, which said, 'go and beg on that corner there' (which he made a point of visibly ignoring) while she crossed the road and took up position outside a convenience store. Red could see immediately what a good position it was for drumming up donations: not only was she by the doors where customers exited with their food, but also beside a row of ATMs. Producing a cap from her back pocket, the young woman sat cross-legged on the ground, and it wasn't long before the contributions started to flow in.

Arms folded and the resentment glowing in his cheeks, Red stood alone on the street corner, unwilling to make the short journey to the ground. He knew that the streets weren't paved with gold, but he'd arrived on them yesterday. Christ, couldn't she cut him some slack? With his foot, he dug at the protruding edge of a crooked flagstone. Part of him knew Gracie was right, not that he would admit it, of course. But it was the way she'd done it; couldn't she see that? The way she'd said it!

Pointedly he looked in the opposite direction to her, out across the Gardens. The sun didn't often shine on Manchester but, when it did, there was no better sight. Red brickwork prospered under its golden touch, and the elongated shadows lent new depth to the landscape of squat bus shelters, overhead tramlines and carpark barriers. Gulls flew overhead, though whether they were departing, arriving from far-off places or had settled there permanently was anybody's guess. Flight, he thought, was a beautiful answer to all these troubles: watching strife with a bird's eye view, drifting over and away, and never through the chaos...

His reverie was broken by a shout, then another. It took him a second or two to realise that it was coming from the direction of the convenience store and a further instant before he registered that the kerfuffle involved Gracie. Without thinking, he hurried across the road. A security guard was remonstrating with her. She was on her feet; the guard's face was right in close to hers, and he was jabbing his finger. Gracie snarled back at him, but her neck craned upwards, and Red saw, in a 'frame' which would remain forever etched in his memory, the sheer physical disparity between the two: his overbearing bulk and her tiny, boyish body. Her vulnerability was like the tinder to an unexpected fire, and Red went tearing in, both hands flying into the guard's chest. The man staggered against the wall of the store from pure surprise rather than being overpowered, and came back at Red, eyes boiling with fury. The young man froze but felt a sudden, savage wrenching of his right arm, pulling him backwards and off balance. He spun; it was Gracie trying to drag him away. He felt the guard's fist against the back of his head – a glance more than a strict connection – and then they were off, haring across the road, as fast as their legs could carry them, almost getting run down by a bus as they went.

'Shit! Me dough!' she said when they finally stopped several streets away. In the rush, she'd left her cap, with everything she'd collected, outside the shop.

'How much was it?'

'I don't fuckin' know. That's a stupid question! I weren't countin' it, were I?'

'Alright,' he said, catching his breath. 'Calm down! At least we survived.'

She snorted. 'Why did you 'ave to go and stick yer beak in?'

He couldn't believe the ingratitude. 'Well, thank you, Red! For saving my life!'

'Life? Give over. I 'ad it covered,' she said. 'Was one o' those fat part-timers. All I know is, I've lost me cap. And I've lost all me potato an' all.'

'Potato?'

'Potato mash – cash.'

'Oh.' He wanted to tell her that calling money potato sounded ridiculous, but the sunlight glinted on the red hair of her capless head, little live wires ready to crackle.

'Weren't just coppers neither. There were notes in there too. Swear down, I'm mad as fuck.'

'Let's go somewhere else, then,' he said warily. 'To beg.'

She glanced at him. 'Come to yer senses, 'ave yer?'

'No, I haven't. But if it will stop you moaning...' He felt sick. 'Just... Don't speak to me. Okay? Don't speak to me.'

When they reached an appropriate spot, he lowered himself to the ground, slowly, eyes fixed on it. Tried not to think of Joe, Dan or Melanie.

'Yer won't get no mash carrying on like that.'

'Told you not to speak to me.'

For a long while, what she'd said was true. Her outstretched hands gradually accumulated the clink and shine of silver coins, while his remained empty, the fingers stubbornly interlocked. Then a wrinkled, well-manicured hand swum into view, and he lifted his head. It was an old lady, bending down with difficulty to offer him some change. He got up quickly, taking the coins and steadying her arm.

'There you go, love,' she said. 'Get yourself a nice cup of tea.'

He hesitated.

Gracie let out a snigger behind him.

'Thank you,' he mumbled finally. 'Thanks a lot.'

After a few hours, the charity of strangers had produced some new 'potato', and they went to spend it in Greggs; Red observed the care that Gracie took to buy for Bart as well as for themselves.

As they arrived back at the canal, the sun had noticeably lowered over the rooftops, and its rays had softened. With the gentle warmth it gave and the pleasure of food entering his grumbling stomach, Red felt the first tingles of contentment since he had run away. His constant fear had relinquished its grip. The indignity of begging was put to one side. The knowledge of what lay back in that old world – his parents, the idea that they might be looking for him, that they might be delighted he'd gone, that they most likely didn't care – dissolved in the smell of meat, potato and pastry that he held straight in his bare hands. Gracie, too, was hungry and ate her food without speaking, full of concentration. It was a companionable silence.

The old man wiped his mouth. He rubbed aggressively at the matted beard, and Red could have sworn he saw pastry flakes and crudely baked canal fish fly up into the air.

'Ah,' he said with heartfelt appreciation. Then he held out his arms and took a deep breath. They were looking out over the canal. Its waters were calm, and the city was quietening down from the hubbub of the day, readying itself for the different hubbub of the night. The clubs were powering up their dance floors, the pubs getting new beers on tap. Gracie had her back to the setting sun, her face in shadow.

She had told Bart about their encounter with the security guard. Now that her mood had improved, she was able to bring some humour to the tale. He laughed a deep booming laugh at each highlight.

'My dear boy,' he said, turning to Red when she'd finished. 'Quite the hero.' He raised a finger. 'And a valuable life lesson.' Cryptically he went on: 'Do you know what it means to be free?'

'Free?'

Gracie rolled her eyes as though she'd heard the line a million times.

'To be free is to be... unpopular,' the old man said with a knowing smile.

'Is that... is that Shakespeare?'

The old tramp laughed fit to burst. 'No, not this one.'

'It's 100% Bartholomew, is wot it is.'

'I don't think I understand,' Red said.

'Oh god. Don't get 'im flippin' started,' said Gracie. 'We'll be 'ere all night!'

'Take a look around,' the man said, his eyes twinkling so that Red couldn't tell whether he was being serious or not. He stretched his arms as wide as they would go. 'Is there anything better than this?'

The young man looked at the man in his tattered clothing, the humble pile of possessions, the fish bones left in their bin-salvaged tinfoil beside a makeshift fire.

'We can do what we want, whenever we want. We answer to no one. No bills to pay, no lawn to keep, no daily grind bending our backs, unlike the rest of this poor city – we have to do... nothing. We are *free*. Do you think they like that?'

'They?'

'The Muggles.' This was Gracie. She threw a stone in the canal, and as it plopped, the water rings spread like they were desperate to escape.

'No one likes us,' he continued. 'We are the great unwanted.'

Hm. There can be other reasons for being unpopular, thought Red a little unkindly. Poor hygiene being one of them.

'But don't we beg from them?'

'We are the reminder of what they could be but will never have the courage to actually be! Think about it, Red. You stepped out of your life.' He looked at Gracie. 'We all did. That took courage. This city is ours, not theirs. They are rootless vagrants here, all their working lives, never realising how fragile their illusion of "security" is, traipsing into those office buildings because they have to, from their treasured commuter homes, then shipping out again, unable to lift their heads. '"What is this life if full of care,'" – he placed a chubby, grimy hand under his chin and lifted it to the horizon – '"We have no time to stand and stare."' He wobbled a little. '*We* have time to stand and stare. Just look at that sunset.'

Red felt sure the old man had been surreptitiously drinking, but he couldn't deny the beauty of the horizon with its spreading red fingertips. Was this freedom? When you were so dependent on charitable giving? Could you have freedom when you were afraid? Because there was no denying the fear in his stomach now – the reprieve had been temporary, and the approach of dusk had set it running again. The prospect of a second night, in the cold and quiet danger of this city, even with his two new companions, filled him with the deepest terror.

When the darkness came, they lay under the bridge, nestled close to its wall, shrouded in their sleeping bags. Red thought back over the day. His mind was a complete jumble. His wrist still ached, like some persistent token of his former life, and it melded with all the other aches that the night presented, physical and mental. Had he done the right thing running away? Sleep was fitful for the other two: Bartholomew breathed heavily; Gracie's exhalations formed a light accompaniment.

Just after midnight, the young man was awoken by the sound of a vicious brawl further down the towpath. He heard the blows landing and resounding across this land of newly declared freedom.

THE STREET

Those first weeks proved to be a great practical education for Red, and he often wondered whether he would have lasted more than a couple of nights without it. At its heart was an appreciation of 'the Street'. It was the place they all inhabited as homeless souls and which they relied upon for survival.

'The Street is your friend,' Bart would say. 'If you're smart and humble, you can find everything you need here. But she is nobody's fool. Never get on the wrong side of her. She likes to bring down those who do.'

Such caprice put her firmly in the realm of old-world deities and their unpredictable passions – anger, vengeance, mercy and grace. A prime mover in human affairs, she was the established recourse for explaining good and ill in a tramp's day. When collections were poor, the Street 'wasn't in a kind mood'; when they were good, her generosity 'knew no bounds'. Divinely she endured while muggles and homeless came and went. She epitomised the harshness of that life, the tumult, the bent for survival – by hook or by crook. With subtle influence, she brought about a change of mindset in her followers, a kind of second sight: of seeing opportunity in the unlikeliest of corners, subsistence in a bare vista or refuge in a makeshift spot.

Daily hunger had washed away Red's resistance to begging like the tide takes care of a sandcastle. After a few days he couldn't have imagined subsisting without it. Gracie taught him further about the locations to beg and those to avoid; he learned about times, and footfall, and their ideal intersection;

about the authorities likely to move you on or leave you be; and everything about the Muggles: their habits, their tells, their street psychology. A short time before, he had been part of their rank. Now he examined them at a remove, as a biologist studies wildlife, perceiving with practice the ones that would give and the ones that might spit at you instead.

It was hard to keep warm, especially when the weather turned. Until he became hardened to it, the cold was of especial torture, numbing all extremities, reaching down through his clothes and gathering in his ribs. The wind had a relentless, biting tongue. He seemed to never stop shivering. His teeth rattled uncontrollably. Bart would bring him close to the fire and wrap an old blanket around him. It stank and was covered in old, crusty food stains, but with that level of discomfort, Red was past caring. He swaddled himself like a baby.

Staying clean was a constant battle. You never realised, until you lost access to regular washing facilities, just how unpleasant the human body smelled after a couple of days and how rashes, sores and other injuries to the skin materialised with ease. It sapped your strength psychologically. You felt like a lesser human being. Within a short space of time, and with Gracie's assistance, he came to know the places you could wash and when. Like her, he dedicated time to it daily; it was an effort, but an important one; he quickly came to respect the self-discipline it demanded and how she'd kept it up for years. She brushed her teeth twice a day as well and avoided the chronic tooth loss which seemed to plague so many of the street community. He followed suit.

Though he would rather jump in the canal than admit it to her, Red admired the diligence with which Gracie seemed to approach living on the Street. It was about more than looking after herself. It was her way of rising above the mire, of demonstrating that the Street *could* be tamed. There was something rebellious about it, an insurrection against the expected order: that being homeless was rock bottom, a broken life, an existence to be pitied or despised for its bankruptcy of ordinary standards. It spoke to him, this project of hers to reclaim respectability against the odds. He understood the feeling of being assigned no meaning or value by others and having to construct it for yourself.

To her credit, she gave advice freely. It was heavily focused on the practical. Here are the charities where you can shower. This is the washroom code for that cafe; if you look clean and don't mither the staff, you'll look like a regular punter using the loo. Those sections of Portland Street get a steady stream of tourists ready to part with their cash. Do not go to Castlefield alone after midnight; avoid the area of Piccadilly Station unless you want to be constantly moved on or locked up by the Gimps. Fixing things, from torn clothes to castaway electrical trinkets (battered old radios, a rusted torch), was a skill of hers he witnessed in frequent action. Her possessions were always well organised, and well looked after.

Bart warned him many a time of the perils of drug use. It was so easy to get drawn into that temporary oblivion, he said; he had seen the best of people succumb. He told stories of tragic demise, of tainted batches, the terrible psychoses and zombified states. Red noticed that, during these speeches, Gracie looked uncomfortable or a little distant. Her head would droop, and she would study the floor. He wondered if she could have been an addict herself in the past. But then surely Bartholomew would have known?

Death seemed an ever-present danger. The young man saw four bodies in the first two months alone. Three were drug overdoses, and none lay in pretty repose; there was blood, vomit and excrement; they were dishevelled, emaciated figures frozen in their last gasp. The fourth was a murder that never got solved. It was an all-over-body beating, and everywhere was bulging, contorted, livid. It was one of the Homeless, but not one they recognised. Gracie said bleakly: 'Bet it's the Serbs wot done that. Probably owed them potato.' She sniffed. 'He won't be begging again.'

Red felt the compulsion to kneel beside the corpses, like he had knelt beside the dead homeless woman all that time ago, out of that strange need to stare death in the face and gauge its touch, but he did not break ranks with Gracie and Bart as they looked on together. The authorities arrived and moved everyone away.

The threat of violence, especially as night drew in, took a long time to get used to. Rumours began to proliferate on the Street that beggars were getting attacked and cut by some unknown miscreant. They would loiter in desolate areas, waiting for a 'bond who was alone, striking when their guard was down. It preyed on Red's mind. He couldn't understand how Bart and Gracie slept with such ease while he lay awake, eyes darting whenever he saw shadows move or heard the scrunch of gravel underfoot. Not that they had switched off to the danger. One time some drunks had come a little too close in the small hours; his companions woke instantly from their slumber and readied themselves for action until the group had passed by.

If a storm were approaching, they would look for an 'empty'. Manchester was not short of derelict buildings as businesses came and went all the time in a constant flurry of rejuvenation. Chinatown had several, and it was in one of those empties that Bartholomew told Red more about his past. It had been a restaurant once, and many of the furnishings were still present, including a mural of a mountain scene with a Mandarin script running down one side. The old man astonished Red by reading the words aloud and translating them.

He might have grown up in Surrey, but Bart's university days had been in Glasgow, where he'd studied philosophy before training as a teacher. Then his travels had begun; after wandering around Europe, he'd ended up in China. A short visit had become a long stay, and he had applied himself to learning the language and trekking round the country. He met and married a Chinese woman and taught English in one of the big cities for 25 years until, quite out of the blue, she found someone else.

Red heard him say a number of times that his true life began with his return to England and the itineracy that led him to Manchester. He had not intended to live out his days as a 'tramp', but the extended period that he'd been out of the country, and the different teaching system over there, meant he had no financial support to fall back on. He could only find occasional lecturing, which paid a pittance; he saw housing officers and completed a universal credit application but was told that 'it would all take time'. It was amazing how quickly the world seemed to close up, clam-like, when it no longer wanted you to be part of its ranks. The answer to that was to limit wholeheartedly your reliance on others and to reappraise the real nature of things. He was now the happiest he had ever been.

Red sensed that a large part of that current happiness was down to Gracie's presence. She continually chided Bart for his well-worn tales and was downright rude to him when in a mood, but he bore it all without complaint, and his red, oily face shone brighter whenever she appeared. There was a rhythm to their thoughts and utterings, and they often finished each other's sentences. They joined forces in lecturing Red about life on the street: one student; two teachers.

Several times Red had been on the verge of asking Gracie how she'd come to be homeless. But she was purposefully closed, a mystery answerable to herself alone. One thing was clear: her burning resolve to stay on the streets and never be housed. This last point was where the views of the old man and young woman intersected perfectly. They had no desire to be imprisoned by rent, a mortgage or a muggle life.

The longer the young man stayed on the streets, the more

he empathised with their view. Sleeping rough could be brutally hard but returning to his former life was unthinkable. It wasn't even a life that belonged to him anymore. Like Bart returning to these shores, it was as though he'd been born the night he'd packed his stuff, closed the front door behind him and taken the bus to the centre. The city had become integral to who he was, nurturing identity and belonging, even among the dirt and the struggle. He, in turn, had become an extension of the city, an incarnation of its spirit, one of the humans in its tapestry. Whether vagrancy as a son of Manchester amounted to freedom, he still didn't know, but it felt like life, as opposed to the death that he'd been living.

Generally, they operated as this established three, and whenever he dwelt on it, Red was freshly surprised that he'd been welcomed into their duo with such readiness. His breakfast meeting with the young woman had been bizarre, to say the least. The old man hadn't batted an eyelid when she'd turned up with a novel homeless in tow; it did all pique the young man's curiosity. But Gracie's nature was so hostile, her tone so confrontational, particularly on anything other than practical talk, that he couldn't ask her why he'd been admitted into their trust. Over time, his curiosity was replaced by gratitude, especially as he realised in hindsight how little he'd contributed at first. He tried here and there to show his thanks – not that it seemed to be sought or noticed. Then a moment came, still less than two months in, when all the faith he had placed in them threatened to be swept away. His money was taken.

V FOR VIP

Red had only resorted to using his funds once, as he considered them an emergency fund, and he'd been incredibly cautious about how he went about it. He found a time when no one was watching and drew a single, crisp note from the wallet stowed in his bag. He rolled it into a fist and plunged it into a trouser pocket.

Gorging himself on a hot bacon roll while out walking on his own was the reward for his subterfuge, and he had never tasted anything so beautiful in his life. There was undoubtedly a selfishness to it, a heightened pleasure from the secrecy. The steaming bread filled the back of his throat as he swallowed, and he let it hang over his stomach before it travelled down. The greasy residue which coated his teeth and tongue lasted for hours, a guilty afterglow as he sat with Gracie and Bart. The salty, buttery memory of the bacon, smothered in red sauce, would not fade, and kept coming to mind, making him smile. He felt such elation. Like he could conquer the world. It was what living on the Street did to you. The process of consumption was transformed. It was memorialisation; it was spiritual fulfilment; it was no longer the take-on of fuel.

Such unalloyed gluttony was bound to have its cost. The next time he checked, the money was gone. He double-checked the bottom of his bag. Tipped out all the contents. A howl of anguish burst from his throat before he could stop himself. Gracie rushed over.

'It was you! Wasn't it?!' he accused, finger jabbing, eyes blazing.

Her eyes narrowed, and like some threatened animal, she produced a snarl.

'Wot? Wot was me?'

Her fists bunched. He thought she might attack. The fury pulsed through him.

'What's going on?' Bartholomew's cultivated voice broke through.

'I don't fucking know! It's 'im! 'E's gone batshit fuckin' crazy!'

Bart turned and looked at Red.

'My... my money. My money's gone! All gone! Which one of you took it?'

The two turned to look at each other: the old man's face a blank frown, the young woman furious but no longer confused.

'Not us, old boy.'

There was an unfriendly edge to his voice – the first time he'd ever caught it from the genial, bearded man – and perhaps a tone of disappointment. True to form, Gracie was less muted. Red had paused in his outburst, and it gave full latitude to her anger: 'D'yer think people are stupid? That we don't all know you've just landed on the streets? That yer might 'ave a couple o' quid stashed? And that every time you went rooting round in yer bag, you weren't checkin' it? We ain't stupid! None of us! 'Cept you. You're the stupid one!'

'Okay, that's enough now,' Bart began.

'No, B! He accused us of takin' 'is money!' She glowered at Red. 'Somebody took yer money. Okay – good. I'm glad. Maybe it'll teach you a lesson. But it wasn't us!' With that, she stormed off, sending a discarded bottle skidding across the ground with one kick.

The next few days were a festival of sulking. Gracie would not even look in Red's direction. She administered sharp tugs to her sleeping bag as she rolled it up in the mornings, was silent other than in Bart's company, and conspicuously guarded her possessions as though Red might exact some tit-for-tat revenge. Bart played a conciliatory role after his initial coldness had dissipated. He told the boy not to worry, that there were no hard feelings and that he was sorry the money had gone. He tried at moments to re-initiate the triangle of dialogue which had characterised their mealtimes before the incident. It didn't work. Gracie was having none of it. But then, neither was Red. The loss of the money still stung terribly. Plus, he needed the distance to think.

He had to reassess whether he trusted his companions at all. Had their reactions to his accusation been some well-choreographed performance? Was it actually his money that had made him so welcome in their group? Would they now jettison him?

Gracie was right that anyone might have seen him checking his money, but he had been so careful. And even then, someone knowing about the money was not the same as them stealing it. There had to be opportunity. Most of the time, he didn't carry the bag around. Generally, Bartholomew watched over their stuff. Could he have taken it? Or left it unattended? Red would never believe the cash had been stolen at night, not when he kept the bag clasped under his head and the slightest footfall had him sitting bolt upright.

Days might go by without them seeing another homeless, but on other days they were inundated with visitors from the community. Bartholomew, in particular, was a popular figure. Would Red have bet against another rough sleeper stealing the cash? No, he would not. While an intense silence cast its pall over them that evening, his mind recapitulated some of the introductions he'd experienced in the past few weeks.

There was Marlo, a middle-aged man who'd fallen foul of his immigration status. He had worked in the UK for more than 20 years, and due to some change in rules that he didn't understand, had no biometric residence permit. Red had registered the man's anger: his lips curled round words; his right eye twitched uncontrollably. He seemed on the verge of mental disintegration, and only Bart's calm tones appeared to settle his ever-churning angst.

Adriana was a Brazilian woman that Gracie got on with. They were unlikely friends: one tall, dark-haired, artistic; the other short, red-haired, tomboyish. One with a lilting Portuguese accent; the other with that flat Mancunian drawl. Adriana wanted to be housed; Gracie would rather die than have a home. But Red soon saw that the Street had no regard for the unlikely; she brought together the opposing corners of humanity, like the gathering of a napkin.

Adriana's story transpired in fragments: a falling out with family; a loss of appetite to study, work, live. The way Gracie was around her surprised him. A depressive air was surely an indulgence that she had no time for. Yet the young woman was transformed: listening patiently, empathising, giving counsel.

An Irishman called Samuel frequented the area around the canals. Job loss was the reason for many figures ending up on the Street, and he was one of the vast contingent who had suffered redundancy during the financial crisis. Originally from Cork, he'd travelled to Manchester in search of work, enduring zero-hour contracts, his phone being stolen, eviction. He had begun to lose his teeth; his forehead was pinkly scarred from a drunken fight; there would be no return to muggle life for him.

'Mind how you go, friends,' he would say as he took his leave of them, patrolling the towpath with his dog for company.

There were many, many others. Every homeless had a tale. Every homeless was on their uppers. Every homeless could have stolen his money. It could have been desperation; it could have been habit. It could have been for the hell of it. Whatever, it was a small leap of imagination to close his eyes and see them poised over his bag, eyes narrowed, fingers searching.

Speculation resolved nothing. The money was gone. Rightly or wrongly, he had accused Gracie and Bart, and the young woman was still angry or hurt, or both. She wouldn't discuss the matter; in fact, she wouldn't talk at all. Gradually the silence was becoming an accepted state of affairs, and that bothered him most of all: that it might continue indefinitely this way and that the comfortable arrangement the three had once enjoyed could be ruined for good.

Oh, it was so difficult to know what to do. If she had taken the money, then this whole bust-up was for the best. They didn't deserve his friendship. But if she *hadn't* taken the money, why then he felt very guilty. After all they'd done for him. He could understand the rage and resentment. So, it all came down to one question: had she taken it?

Gracie was different to Melanie. The streetgirl showed every feeling in her face, whereas his classmate had always had a game in play, hidden behind dark eyes, so that he couldn't pinpoint the sleights of hand. Red wondered what Melanie was doing now. Had she been shocked by his departure? Was she upset by it? Or had he rapidly moved out of her thoughts? Was she now focused on some other boy?

Red had promised himself never to rely on another person again. Never to be dragged into friendships, loyalty, emotional ties. What were Gracie and Bart to him? He barely knew them. That was the truth of it. His life was going to be one of solitude, of eschewing all commitment. He would never get married, never have children. He would never love anyone. Ever. He would never make himself so vulnerable. Families were a road to pain. He merely had to think of his parents to know what a mistake that could be.

With a hurried glance, he sought out his bag. There it was, leaning on a wall between the rucksacks of his two companions, Gracie's at a slight remove as though she couldn't bear their possessions to touch. Everything he owned – always ready, always packed. These people did not matter. His life alone might as well start now. Get up from where you're sitting this minute and keep on walking! He had abandoned his mother and father; there should be no hesitation here.

'Why is life so hard?' he griped under his breath.

The next morning, Red rose early and wandered off. His mission had formed clearly overnight, and he walked with purpose along Tib Street, weaving through the scaffolding that fronted a row of buildings. Begging for hours in the places he knew well, at the times that worked best, he collected a decent amount of notes and spare change. He bought food for them: more than normal, making sure that it included a steak slice which he knew was Bart's favourite.

A flurry of panic gripped him as he approached because they were nowhere to be seen, and his heart lurched at the thought that he might not know where they'd gone, but then he spotted that they'd moved 150 yards down the towpath.

After handing out the fruits of his labour, he sat in the now customary silence.

'A gimp came by,' Gracie said at length. 'Told us lot to move on.'

'There's a council building that overlooks the spot we were occupying,' added Bart. 'Well, from a certain angle. Must be a VIP coming. Wouldn't do to see the local riffraff living it large outside the windows.'

'So we flicked 'im the V. V for VIP, right?' She chuckled and met Bart's eye. 'Then we moved down 'ere.'

Red nodded, looking about him as though inspecting the new territory.

And that was all it took. Everything reverted to how it had been before. Gracie spoke with him as she always had – full of spleen and swearwords – and no signs were left of the storm that had blown in or the subsequent rebuild.

LIGHT

Another way of procuring money was through honest toil. It would be wrong to think that living on the streets meant no chance of work entirely. You had to be careful not to get ensnared in criminal activity, and what you earned would never be dependable or enough to put a roof over your head. But there was a whole underground economy of cheap, unskilled labour. A lorry needed loading, a yard wanted clearing, a set of toilets had to be swabbed after an incident-filled night at a local club. The Homeless were not to be trusted, were often weak and in poor health, but they – generally – had a pair of arms and a pair of legs, would accept the lowest wages and were employed task by task without workers' rights and in cash.

One day, the owner of a takeaway came. His name was Aziz. He needed someone to come and help with stocktaking and cleaning. Gracie must have worked for him before because she showed none of her usual caution about Sharks and Wolves.

'I'll do it,' she said, jumping to her feet.

Naturally, Red volunteered as well. The man looked him up and down with a non-committal eye and said, 'I need one. You,' he pointed at the young man. 'Come with me.'

Gracie was a little put out, but no doubt understood that his size and strength, in lugging boxes around and scrubbing down walls, put him above her in the hiring.

'You go,' she said.

Red gave her a reassuring nod in response: whatever he earned he wouldn't be keeping for himself.

They picked their way across some wasteland under development, pigeons scattering at their approach, and down a couple of alley turns, until they reached the establishment.

'What is your name?'

'Red.'

'I am Aziz. Don't worry,' he said, smiling. 'Some people not pay well. I pay well. I like to help.'

The front of the takeaway was tidy and clean enough, with lacquered benches for customers to wait on and a simple serving counter, but the 'back of shop' was a state: dirty, with stock piled up everywhere. Red noticed carpeted stairs with heavily worn treads, which led to the upper floor, presumably where Aziz lived.

The man observed his glance and said with an emphatic wag of his finger, 'Don't go up.' A look at his watch. 'Takeaway open in three hours. Move these boxes,' he indicated. 'Put them there.'

'There' was full of crates.

'You need move them first. Clean the floor.'

There was a large clock on one wall. After an hour, Aziz came in to see how Red was progressing. 'You can go more faster. You are young and strong,' he said. His genial manner had disappeared. The boy's back and arms ached. He wasn't used to the physical demand, but he kept quiet.

A further hour-and-a-half trickled by before the man returned. Red had made substantial headway, and Aziz was impressed to hear that he had reordered stock based on the expiry date, combining boxes which were partially full. 'Good,' he said. 'Thank you.' Then mysteriously: 'I go out. Do not go anywhere. Do not go upstairs. I pay you when I come back.'

'Okay.'

Red watched as the leather shoes mounted the first few stairs; he hollered up in his native tongue. Although the boy didn't hear it, there must have been some reply as the man looked satisfied.

Time advanced: half an hour, an hour. Still no sign of his

return. After an hour and fifteen minutes, while the young man had his back turned, there was a creaking sound and the gentle thud of footfall. Whoever had been upstairs was descending. Red spun round and saw that it was a woman of about his own age – a strikingly beautiful woman.

The woman's hair was a dark, mesmerising waterfall; it shone in the gloom as if an unseen light had touched it from crown to shoulders.

'Who are you?'

The vagrant swallowed. He felt shy and utterly embarrassed by his dishevelled appearance.

'I'm Red. Aziz hired me to do some work for him.'

'Aziz is my father.' The nose and cheekbones were classically elegant, the eyebrows well-shaped above two curious eyes. Her command of English was impeccable, an accent showing only on the r's.

'Are you from the canal? My father brings people from there.' There were two red plastic stools in a corner of the storeroom. She set them out. 'Please, sit. Would you like something to drink?'

'I shouldn't.'

'I'm making you my guest.'

'Some water, then. Please.' He had been sweeping. He rested the broom against a wall. Self-consciousness inhibited his every movement like he was a walking apology: gaucheness in his streetboy gait, discomfort from his sorry hygiene. He sat on the stool.

'I'm getting myself an orange squash. I'm sure you'd like one of those.' Then: 'The people my father brings are homeless.'

'Yes.'

'Why are you homeless?'

'Well, I ran away from home.'

'Because you hated your parents?'

He didn't know the answer to that himself. 'I was unhappy.'

'Are you happy now?'

'Some bits better, some bits worse.'

She sipped her drink. 'So why not go back?'

'No, I couldn't do that.' He smiled an awkward smile. She was very direct, and for a guest, he was getting quite an interview.

'Sometimes, I would like to run away. A million miles from here. But then I change my mind.' She glanced around the room. 'It looks better than it did. My father will return soon. Please don't tell him I spoke with you,' she said.

'Because I'm homeless?'

'Not exactly.' She began to climb the stairs, that poised, feminine tread.

'Wait. What is your name?'

'Noura.'

'Nou-ra.'

'It means "light". I am Syrian,' she said. 'Have you heard of the war?'

'A bit.' The truth was: almost nothing.

She leaned on the banister. 'We are from Bashariyah. A town near Latakia. My brother was arrested, so we came here, my father and me. We have family in the UK; we used to come here when I was a child. I schooled for four years. My mother is still at home. She wouldn't leave, not without my brother. But it is over three years now. No word. She goes to the city prison all the time; she has been beaten by the guards; she will not give up.'

'I'm sorry. That can't be easy for you.'

'Thank you. What is it like?' she asked. 'Being homeless?'

'Cold,' he said. 'You get used to it.'

'I am homeless, too, I suppose. I miss my home. The way things were. Most of all, I miss a time. The war has made me time-less.'

'When will you go back?'

'I won't.'

Red studied his drink. Her beauty made him ache. He had no sexual experience, no experience even of girls liking him. Any school crush had led nowhere fast, and the whole thing of boys and girls 'dating' was another source of alienation for him, along with the rest of the misery he'd felt before he ran away. Melanie might have been the chance for him to gain experience, but her personality had always put him off. Plus, he'd never felt that she was interested in him in 'that way'. She'd wanted him to confide things; she'd wanted to monopolise his company; she'd wanted to shock him sometimes and rouse emotions, but there was no indication that she wanted to be touched or held.

There was the sound of the front door opening. Aziz had returned. Noura smiled, some unknown thought playing at her lips.

'You have sweeping to do,' she said and hurried upstairs.

KING

Gracie and Bart were waiting outside the takeaway when he finished.

'Red, my dear fellow!' Bartholomew folded and patted one of his thickly stuffed tobacco roll-ups. He'd caught the sun. His forehead was glowing, as was the bridge of his nose.

''Ow was it, then?' asked Gracie.

'Was fine. Had me clearing stuff, stacking crates. Some broom action.' I met an incredibly beautiful woman called Noura, he thought.

'Could 'ave yer tickling ferrets, for all I care. Long as there's some silver at the end of it.'

'There's gratitude for you.'

'I did well with the cap,' she said. 'Me and B made some signs. I was pushing signs over at St Peter's. Take a look.'

Red held one of the signs they'd crafted. It read: 'I AM YOUNG AND HOMƎLƎSS. PLS GIVƎ WHAT YOU CAN.'

'Why are the E's backwards?'

'Make 'em feel sorry for my lack of education. Gotta make it look real, don't you? For the Muggles.'

'But you are homeless.'

She sighed. 'Look, Einstein. Who knows better 'ow to bum, you or me?'

'Why do you always use that word?'

'It's the right word!'

'It sounds, I don't know. Wrong.'

She laughed. ''Ow much did the Arab give yer then? For the work?'

He brought out the two notes and dropped them into her cap. She grinned. 'There'll be some fine dining tonight,' she said.

Bartholomew snorted. They turned to him.

'And wot are you putting in, B?' Her eyes shone like she was indulging a pet.

'You can't put a price on company. I bring wisdom and erudition.'

'That ain't legal tender round 'ere, friend.'

'Anyway,' said Red. 'What are you doing here?'

'We're gunna meet someone,' Gracie answered.

'Who?'

'You'll see. You'll like 'im. He's a 'bond. Just like us.'

They walked along Portland Street, then headed for the Chorlton Street bus station. It wasn't quite the ugliest building in Manchester, but it couldn't have been far off. It was more concrete than glass and had a peculiar canopy that ran around it like a skirt. Inside, the floor was dirty from all the passenger traffic.

After half an hour a coach arrived. The passengers descended onto the tarmac. Last to step down was a curious-looking man. The first thing Red noticed about him was the tattoo of a roaring lion sprawled across his forearm and how the man's sleeve was rolled up, putting it on full display. He was carrying a bag on his shoulder. His waist was tightly cinched with a belt. He had his head held high, and his chest pushed out, as though he had to dominate his surroundings.

'Hello, Gracie,' he said.

'Hello, Darren.' She went up and embraced him. 'I got word you was comin'.'

Dusk was on its way, and they were gathered round a fire. The man Darren was holding court. Gracie looked happy in his company; she seemed to hang off his every word. Bart was in his fishing chair, as usual, resembling a fallen angel, quietly smoking.

The visitor turned to Red. His eyes moved quickly, weighing up what was in front of him. 'What's your story, lad?'

'Same as everyone else's. Give or take.'

'How long you been on the streets?'

Gracie laughed. 'Our Darren can always spot a newbie.'

'I'm not that new.'

'We were all new once.' Darren smirked. 'It's nothing to be ashamed of, fella. Welcome to the Street, however long you've been here. One thing's for sure, you haven't been out in this city as long as Gracie here, and Bart neither. I'm sure they're looking after you.'

'Oh, this lad can look after himself, don't you worry,' Bart spoke up. He sucked on the bitter end of his roll-up, the hand steady.

'Red's workin' in that takeaway down there on Dale Street,' Gracie explained to Darren. 'Wot's the name again?'

'Aladdin's.'

'Never heard of it.' He gave a short, sharp laugh. 'But then it's a little while since I've been here.'

'Where are you from?' Red asked though he had no particular interest in the answer.

'No fixed abode,' he grinned. 'Now there's a thing.'

'We're all no fixed abode,' said Gracie. 'Stop kidding round.'

'I've come up from Birmingham. Spent the last year or so there. I move around. It's a while since I was in Manchester. Can't believe how much this one has grown up.' He nodded at Gracie.

She laughed.

'There was a guy I knew there. In Birmingham. Proper Brummie, you know. Met him first day I went down. He was a good lad. But he couldn't lay off the Spice. It took him in the end.'

Each head lowered at what was a familiar story.

'Have you ever seen someone die of it?' he asked. His eyes glinted mysteriously in the half-light. 'I found him. Not a pretty sight. Not something I'd want you young people seeing.'

The man couldn't have been all that old himself, Red thought. Though it was difficult to tell sometimes. He gave the impression, like Gracie, of an individual completely at home on the Street, as if he had long ago mastered 'the game': he was not one of those gaunt, beaten down figures so often seen shambling through the city. Taken out of his surroundings he could easily have passed for a muggle; it was only his gait that might mark him out. At one point he stood up to poke the fire in its metal drum, and Red had observed his walk, the kind that a certain type of homeless had – confident, sharp, the feet moving quickly over the ground, like rolling tank tracks. They were 'Kings of the Street'. Darren had that way of moving, and it made Red dislike him even more.

It was a misplaced confidence, of course. The Street was indomitable; she bent to no king. Anyone of them could be dead within a year, including this Darren, and it never paid to forget that. The young man stared at the fire, thoughts wandering to what the future held. He turned to look at Bart: hopefully the old man would last a long time. He glanced at Gracie: one day, her time would come too. Finally, he thought of himself.

Death would reveal its substance to each of them in turn, be it cessation, continuity or a fresh commencement. It would choose the order; they would not go at the same time; one would go first, leaving the others behind, to grieve and remember. The same applied to his mother and his father, whether he saw them again or not; to Dan, Joe, Melanie, Marlo, Adriana, Samuel, this Darren... Every person on the earth would depart at some point until every living human had transitioned, in a precise sequence six billion long.

''E's always daydreamin'.' It was Gracie speaking, and Red realised that he was the centre of attention.

'I'm going for a walk.' He headed away down the towpath. Rain was threatening, and he hoped that was all it would do. He would hate to be forced back to the shelter of the bridge where Darren still held court. 'The man is a complete twat,' he muttered under his breath. 'Why can't you see that, Gracie?'

A swing of his arm, a stone meeting the water. He thought of Noura. Wondered what she might be doing right now. His imagination decided unashamedly that she must be in a hot bath. She would be soaking in its sumptuousness, that dark mane of hair – as dark as the canal – fanning out behind her pale neck and shoulders. She had soft skin, scented, clean, exotic, a thousand miles from the dirty touch of a homeless boy. She was warmth, safety, a covered sky. Everything he didn't have.

'You should come back under the bridge, my boy. Looks like rain.' Red turned to find the solicitous face of Bartholomew suddenly close and watchful. His beard was looking especially unkempt, and his hair needed a decent cut, the white curls springing away from the crown.

'Ah. It might hold off for a bit.' Inadvertently Red glanced in the direction of Gracie and Darren.

'She knows him from way back,' Bart said.

'Hmm.'

'Before she knew me.' There was a pause while the old man fumbled in his tobacco pouch. 'I think he met her when she first ran away from her foster parents.'

Inside, despite himself, Red felt a little sting of jealousy that Gracie should be a fan of Darren at all, that their group of three could end up being a group of four.

'What about her real parents?'

Bart's eyes were fixed on some part of the horizon, touching the tips of the high-rises. 'She told me once. Her story.'

'She has a story?'

'Everyone has a story. Just some are darker than others.' He half-smiled. 'And hers is one of the darkest I've heard.'

'I see.'

'She will tell you, I think. When she's ready.'

'No. I think she hates me.'

The old man laughed, the grime crinkling around his eyes.

'"In time, we hate that which we often fear."'

'Shakespeare?'

'Antony and Cleopatra.'

'So you're saying she fears me?'

'Not exactly.'

'Then what?'

He shrugged, though not uncomfortably. 'She is vulnerable. She puts on a big show, but underneath the surface...' He trailed off.

There was a noise behind them. A lone duck. Its beak prodded the grass verge. Bart was suddenly thoughtful. 'Gracie needs someone kind in her life. Good people. If Darren keeps hanging around, I will tell him.'

'Saying what?'

'That he's "persona non grata".'

'I don't think that's wise, Bart. He looks the type you shouldn't cross. I'd stay out of it. Gracie will realise what a tool he is soon enough.' Even as he spoke, Red registered the doubt in his voice. He hoped the old man would listen. He read something disturbing beneath Darren's controlled veneer, like a sudden capacity for violence.

Then Bart said: 'It's time I told you something. About my story. I only told you half.'

'Sure.'

'I had a son. Have.' At this, he stared into the distance. 'I left him behind in China, with his mother. And her inamorato.'

Red wasn't sure what to say.

'So what do you think of me now, Red? The great abandoner. Abandoning his own son.'

'It was your wife who found someone else.'

Bart considered. 'A wife doesn't find a lover out of the blue. Not truly. There were other... reasons.' He ran his fingers through his beard. 'A child is not enough to save a failing marriage. Another person is never enough for the problems within yourself. I was in a prison. When she found someone else, that was the prison door being opened. For both of us.'

'You could still... you could still go and see him. If you wanted to. You're not her husband. But you're still his father.'

He shook his head. 'The time has gone, my dear fellow. He will have his own life. I would bring him nothing but shame or, what is worse, indifference. That is *my* fear.'

'I doubt that.'

'I lack courage, you see. Always have.'

'Come on now, Bart.'

'You don't know the half of it.'

The conversation had moved so quickly and into territory the young man felt unsure how to handle. He had never known the man given to self-pity; he was the character who always had some wisdom to impart, a dry comment, a classical reference to remind them that the fundamentals of life never changed. And here he was, tearing himself apart. Red was shocked to see the man's eyes gleaming as he turned to look at him, waters that must have been held back for some time. 'I have tried,' he said. 'I swear, Red.'

'I know.'

Rough, swollen, and with dirt lining the nails, his hand rested on the metal rail which guarded the canal. The young man patted the hand but could find no words.

BRACELET

Every few days, Aziz would come; with Red having proven himself, the takeaway owner had decided to leverage the cheap labour as much as he could. 'I help you, you help me,' he shrugged. 'The laws in this country, I do not understand. You want work. I want worker. You come; I pay. Everybody happy.'

The next couple of times, the man was always on the premises, and there was no sign of Noura. The father did not call up; she did not come down; there was not even the creak of a floorboard to suggest a presence.

At last, an afternoon came that Aziz did go out, and less than ten minutes later, Red recognised a familiar tread. His heart banged, and his mouth was dry. Once again, it was the river of black tresses, freshly brushed, which drew his eye. She was wearing a long-sleeved, turquoise blouse; it was tighter to her body than the previous clothing, and as she rested her hand on the stair banister, he saw the close contour and upwards bulge where the slim ribcage met her breast. His head swirled.

'I have something for you,' he said and brought out a daisy bracelet. He had found the daisies growing in the corner of a car park, where cars swung through the exit, and their tyres stopped short of a patch of grass.

Although Noura smiled, she put the bracelet in her pocket rather than on her wrist. It wasn't what Red had hoped for. He had wanted blushes, a coquettish embarrassment, and in his wildest dreams, a thank you that might lead to a kiss. Indifference was too strong a word, but there was no delight.

The young woman was not alive to his disappointment, which knocked his confidence further.

'Do you read?' she asked.

I can't read you, he thought. But just shook his head.

'I saw a homeless man, once, reading a book. Why do you not read?'

'I don't know.' We're not all the same, that's why. 'I never have.'

'But you come from a country which has great writers.'

'You mean Shakespeare. You'd get on with my friend, Bartholomew. Never stops quoting him.'

'There are other writers. I like Thomas Hardy. I studied English literature at school. Have you heard of Hardy?'

'Yes,' he lied.

'He wrote about love.'

Red's heart lifted, and he looked at her, but she did not reciprocate. 'And not just daisy chains,' she added, giving a little laugh. She did turn to look at him then, but suddenly he was the one avoiding glances, feeling the smart of her comment.

'Did he now? And what did Hardy say?'

'That it isn't at all where you think,' she said.

'Why?'

'I don't know. It just isn't.' She sighed. 'My favourite book is Wuthering Heights. It's by Emily Bronte.'

'Is that about love too?'

'How can you not know this? You're English. Yes. Love. And hate.'

'Hm.'

'It says that the depths of hate are as deep as the depths of love. Have you ever hated anyone?'

My parents, sometimes, he thought. Not 'hate', as such, but then how deep did hatred go?

'There are times I hate what my life is,' she said. 'What it's become. I hate being powerless. But I have no one to hate.'

'You could hate the people who started the war in your country.'

'A waste of time.'

'And what do you think of my country?'

'Your country?' she giggled. 'What do I think of your country? You sound like you're the king.'

'You could be queen.'

She giggled again and – finally – gave him an encouraging glance. 'Thank you, kind sir. How can you be a king, though, if you don't have a palace?'

'I'm a wandering king. The whole land is my palace.'

'I see. Other than this,' she said, 'what do you do all day?'

'Nothing much. I have some companions.'

'Knights of the Round Table.'

'Not many knights...'

'Who are they?'

'An old man,' he said. 'And a woman.'

'An old woman?'

'No, she's about the same age as me.'

'What does she look like?'

'Erm. Ordinary.'

'Do you smoke?' she asked. He was surprised to find that she had produced a packet of cigarettes and a lighter. 'Have you ever tried?'

She gave him one and lit it. He copied the way she held hers, but it still sat very awkwardly between his fingers. He suppressed a cough. Her grip was well-practised. He had never watched any woman smoke before; he had never realised how feminine the act could be. How transformed Noura was. Her eyes expressed tiny sparks of pleasure as she inhaled, her mouth enveloped the end of the cigarette delicately. She crossed her legs and rested one hand on her thigh.

After a minute, she rose. She tugged open the back door to the takeaway.

'My father doesn't know that I smoke. But all the girls do. Well, did. Back home.' She paused. 'None of their fathers knew either.'

She half-laughed. 'Rebellion begins at home.' He approached behind her. A swirl of smoke came up and wreathed the two of them. He was much closer to her now than he'd been before, close enough to touch her shoulders with his hands. As though knowing and resisting, Noura stepped out of the back door and into the alleyway. He followed, and she glanced around with caution.

'Is it because I'm homeless?'

'Is what?'

'You don't want to be seen with me.'

'You're a man.'

'A man?'

'Yes. My father wouldn't approve.'

'Then why did you come downstairs?'

She didn't answer. A couple of minutes passed; she was almost at the end of her cigarette.

Then she said: 'You're easy to talk to.' She considered a little longer. 'You're different. You're not part of my world.'

The alleyway was narrow, and their voices resounded faintly against the red brick. 'I hate my father sometimes,' she said. 'He wants to control everything. Losing my brother has made him ten times worse. And then coming here!' She rolled her eyes and shook her head.

'Why don't you run away then?'

She laughed. 'No money. Not knowing where the next meal is coming from. No shelter. I couldn't do it.' She laughed again. 'I admire you, honestly,' and he could see from her eyes that she was being genuine, 'but it would be a prison for me. I mean. How would I wash my hair?' A final laugh, then she fell serious. 'Besides. What would my father do?'

'This is last time,' said Aziz, and it took a few seconds for the statement to sink in. They were standing together at the back door of the takeaway, by the bins overflowing with trash. Red felt the panic in his chest.

'You... you won't need me again? There are still things to–'

'No. I go away. For a long time.'

Red stopped himself saying: 'And Noura?'

The man went to the front of the shop. Twenty or so minutes passed. He showed no sign of leaving. Then, just as the young man was giving up hope, he heard Noura calling her father. After a brief exchange, Aziz left the premises.

'I told him to get something for me.'

'He said this is the last time he'll need me.'

'Yes.'

'You know?'

She nodded.

'What's going on? Have I done something wrong?'

'I'm getting married,' she said.

He was too stunned to respond. Then at length, he said simply: 'I don't understand.'

'We can't go back to Syria. But we will go to Jordan. We have relatives there. My father has found someone for me.'

'Found someone?'

'An engineer. He comes from a good family.'

'But you're too young to get married.'

'Why?'

'You just are.' A pause. 'So, you're leaving. Just like that.'

'Yes. Next week.'

'Next week?' There was no way she hadn't known about this for a while. The broom Red was holding felt rough and clumsy in his hands as he continued to sweep while speaking. The movements became quicker, angrier. 'And what about love?'

'What about it?'

'I thought you read books about it. Hardy. Bronte. How can you love this engineer? You haven't even met him.'

'I think you can learn to love anyone. If they're a good person.'

'Bet you wouldn't say that about a tramp.' He wouldn't look at her. He felt humiliated: this one person who had actually spoken to him like another human being had been keeping a secret from him all this time. He felt betrayed by what was happening, and at that moment, he wanted her to suffer terribly for it. He wanted her wracked with guilt that he was a nothing, a nobody! In everybody's eyes, including hers. This proved it. He had nothing. He stank. Was a living embodiment of failure. Even to her, he meant absolutely *nothing!*

'Make-believe is nice,' she said. 'But there are books, and then there is life. Book love isn't–'

'What if this engineer guy isn't a good person? What if he's horrible?'

'My father has chosen him.'

'Big deal.'

'My father knows what is important to me. What is in my best interest.'

'He doesn't even know you smoke.'

Noura folded her arms and turned away bitterly. 'All I've ever had,' she said, 'is down to him. Who are you to... Who *are* you?' She looked him up and down; there was contempt in her gaze. 'You're in no position to lecture me.'

The cuffs of his sweatshirt, one of the two that he owned, had started to fray, and he tugged at the left cuff self-consciously before deciding to abandon the movement. It was what it was. He was what he was.

'I have something for you,' she said, her voice lowered. Noura's hand went to the pocket of her jeans, and she pulled out a folded piece of paper. 'I had a look online. It's from a jobs board. It is a list of jobs. Ones that you could do.'

He set the broom to one side, went over and took the outstretched paper.

'You're better than this,' she said. Then she kissed him on

the cheek, and he was momentarily dazzled by the soft scent. 'Goodbye,' she said and went upstairs. It didn't seem possible for matters to suffer such an abrupt end, measured in seconds rather than days, but it was the last time he saw her.

NOWT

It was early morning before dawn had fully broken, though its grey inception was announced in the slivers between buildings. A seagull landed a few feet from Red and busied itself with an upended takeaway box. Itinerants of the skies, migrants from distant lands, the gulls flocked to Manchester from the Irish Sea, circling, searching, hanging on the winds. He wondered at the journey that this one had made before descending to earth for its scrap of food. The bird's head became trapped in the box; it flapped and jumped, shaking it off. He wondered whether one had ever travelled all the way from Jordan. He didn't even know whether Jordan had shores, a coast, blue waters... It was a name and nothing more.

The piece of paper unfolded with ease, crackling as he straightened it. There were contact names, phone numbers, email addresses. A mixture of odd jobs, from cleaning to leafleting, no qualifications needed.

Half of him felt insulted, the other half felt moved. The list was a 'pay-off', a way to assuage her conscience that she was abandoning him, but it was a gift as well, a human kindness nestling between his fingertips. She'd gone to the trouble of putting it together. She wasn't abandoning him because there was nothing to abandon. Did he think she owed him something because of a few conversations?

Red made sure he was alone before he tore the sheet of paper into pieces and scattered them over the canal. Their whiteness glittered before the current took them. Then he leaned against the rail and contemplated the surface, which felt suddenly like a canvas of the future; the moment was a crossroads, a decision knowingly taken, for good or ill.

'Morning.' It was a man's voice. Red turned to see Darren smirking. 'Gracie asked me to be here early.'

'Oh. Why?' With the others asleep, there was more opportunity for their hostility to show itself.

'She probably wants to do something together.'

A minute of silence passed. It should be crystal clear, thought Red, that he didn't want to speak with him; he rolled up his sleeping bag and stowed it in his rucksack. 'I'm going for a shower,' he said finally. He would get it at Refuge House or the gym that he had sneaked into regularly by tailgating members.

'You know something,' Darren began. Red noticed him pushing up his sleeves, and the roaring lion was suddenly visible, as it had been the day before. 'You won't last.'

'Meaning?'

'Here. On the Street. You don't have what it takes.'

'And you do?'

'Yes. I do. I was practically born under one of these here bridges. I know exactly what it takes.' His lips had curled into a strange smile, baring his teeth as he spoke. 'If it weren't for the others, you'd already be fucking gone. And one day – one day when you're least expecting it – they'll up and leave. You'll be on your fucking lonesome.'

'I don't think they will.'

'You're a child.' A malicious twinkle in the eye. 'You have no idea.'

'Why are you here?'

'I'm here *because*.'

'Because what?' The anger of Noura's rejection still burned in Red, and it fired a certain recklessness. 'Because you like bigging yourself up? Because Birmingham got sick of you?'

'Because *nothing*. That's something you'll learn. There is no why out there. Only survival.'

'Yeah, yeah. Heard it all before, mate.'

'There's life and death and the tiny fucking line in-between. Whether you wake up each morning. Or not.'

'Leave Gracie alone.' He stepped closer to the other man. His heart was banging. 'You're not welcome. Leave her be.'

'I say who I spend time with.' It was Gracie, a furious scowl spread across her face.

Red opened his mouth and closed it again.

Darren sneered and left.

'Wot the fuck is goin' on?' she asked.

Red wouldn't look at her.

'Darren was in Care with me. I owe 'im.'

'Still. Doesn't stop him being a prick.' He was intrigued. 'Why do you owe him?'

'It doesn't matter.' She paused. Pointed in the direction of the takeaway. 'Who is she, then?'

'Who's who?'

'Who d'yer think?' Gracie snorted.

'Stop trying to change the subject.'

'D'yer like 'er?'

'Noura. That's her name.'

'Whatever.'

'I... I don't want to talk about it. Tell me why you owe Darren.'

She shrugged. 'I told yer. I was in Care with him.'

'And?'

'I was in a bad place. I couldn't even speak hardly. He helped me back.'

'You hardly speaking! That'll be the day.'

'You didn't know me back then.'

'Okay. I get it. But he's so up himself. You must have noticed. I mean, who has a lion tattoo? He thinks he's king of the jungle, doesn't he? Survival of the fittest. All that crap. And you lap it up!'

'Well. Least I didn't give 'im a daisy bracelet.'

Red's head snapped round. 'So you were spying on me! Thanks a bunch. Well, you'll be glad to hear – she's... she's getting married.' He glanced at Gracie, expecting her to laugh at his expense, but her face was serious, considering.

'Huh? Who's she marryin'?'

'Some engineer bod. She's off to some country about a thousand miles away.'

'Wow. She sure wants to get away from you.' She pulled a face. 'Are yer sad?'

'Bit.'

'It's good she's gone.'

'I'm not bothered either way.'

'Listen, she ain't interested in yer. She don't see you as one of her... Well. You're from different worlds.'

'How do you know?'

'I know.'

'Because I'm homeless?'

'Nah,' she said. 'Not everythin's 'bout being 'omeless. It's where she's from that rules you out.' She paused, and for once, there was kindness in her voice. 'Yer a child of Manchester. You deserve better.'

'That's a cliche. I'm the lowest of the bloody low.'

'Wot, 'cos yer don't got money?'

'I don't have anything.'

'That ain't true.' Gracie bridled, a little hurt. 'Besides. You could 'ave nowt. Not even the clothes you stand up in. But you'd still have summat.'

'Thanks. You're going soft.'

'That's true of anyone, though, innit? We're all born wi' something.'

'Well,' he said, considering. 'You do too. You're special, you know.' Red meant what he said.

Gracie had none of Noura's abilities or instincts to conceal, and confusion burst immediately over her face. He was shocked to see a blush rising up her throat.

SHARIN' IS CARIN'

The young woman quickly moved into street talk, avoiding Red's gaze. 'I saw someone get proper set on yesterday.' She pointed into the distance towards Piccadilly Gardens.

'Shame it wasn't yer best pal, Darren.'

'Oi.'

Red rolled his eyes. He felt cold. As Gracie talked, he dug in his bag for his other jumper. It had slid to the bottom and was nestled under the book on human pathology he had brought from home. Still, he lugged it everywhere without ever opening it. He paused, conscious of its weight and the memories it stirred of pre-street life and morbid inquiry.

''Appened down Market Street,' she went on. 'Broad daylight it were. Poor bloke.'

'Who did it? Was it that nutter – the one who's attacking us homeless?'

'Nah, I've told yer that's a myth anyhow.' She tutted. 'Were a crew 'avin' a go. No standard fight neither. Three of 'em jumped 'im. One of 'em full-on lamped 'im, then they all started eggin' on the lad. They left 'im there, then the Gimps arrived. They called the Cross out.'

'Jesus.'

'That Marek was one of 'em.'

'What?'

'Yeah. Told yer not to get mixed up with 'im. Now there's a fuckin' nutjob. I heard the guy who got beat up owed money. Lucky it wasn't worse. The moneylending crews, they don't normally just land a few punches. Often, they take a finger, or worse.'

'Take a finger?'

'Yeah. One holds yer hand down, the other brings out the cleaver.'

Red grimaced.

'This lad I know said there's been a couple o' times people have been proper in debt. You know wot 'appens then.' She drew a finger across her throat, which he was relieved to see had returned to a normal colour. 'Get iced. 'E said they took one down Canal Street.'

Manchester did have a Canal Street. But that wasn't her meaning; Red looked at the murky waters that lay in front of them and couldn't help seeing again the image of a floating corpse, blood congealed at the back of the head where the victim had been struck.

He had put his spare jumper on now. He went to close the rucksack; light fell on the cover of the pathology book, making the sharp edges shine. Would she understand?

'I used to read about death,' he said.

Gracie almost choked. A strand of red hair came down over her face, and she tucked it behind one ear. 'That's probably the weirdest thing anyone's ever said to me.'

'Are you congratulating me?'

'Nah.'

'I have this book. I found it in the school library. It's a pathology book.'

'Wot's that?'

'You've never heard of pathology?'

'No.'

'It's the study of dead bodies.'

'Oh. Cutting 'em up and stuff.'

'Yes. Cutting 'em up and stuff.'

'Yer a freak.'

'I brought it with me. It's in here.' He reopened the rucksack.

'Come on then. Gi' us a look. Eff all else to do.'

Gracie took the book in her hands and began to leaf through the pages until she came to a section on drowning. Pictures of victims leapt out. She studied them, ignoring the print. Watching her in profile, Red wondered at the young woman's thoughts; she lifted her head and gazed into the distance, gripping a page between her forefinger and thumb.

'D'yer think they suffered?' she asked after a minute.

'I don't know. Do you mean from dying itself or from knowing it was the end?'

'Wot's that thing they say about yer last look? How it's printed on yer eyes or somethin'? The last person you look at.'

'I dunno. Never heard that.'

'I was the last person my sister looked at.'

Red stared at her, but she looked away. There was a long silence. She went back to turning the pages.

'Here, I wanted to ask you something,' he said. 'If I were to have a steady job–'

'That Noura still wouldn't be interested.'

'No, no... it's a question I wanted to ask you. If I had a steady job, if we could manage to have a roof over our heads – you, me, Bart – what do you think?' What Darren had said before bothered Red more than he'd care to admit. That he wouldn't make it. That the three of them wouldn't tough it out together.

'A steady job?'

'Yeah.'

'Somewhere to live?'

'You, me, B.'

'Couldn't afford it.'

'I think we could, somehow.'

'No. You can do it if yer want. But not me.'

'Why not?'

'It's not for me, that. This is where I belong. 'Ere. Where people like me belong.'

'I'm people like you.'

'You can do that. Seriously. If yer want. But I won't be coming with you. I am not homeless; the Street is my 'ome.'

'I don't understand, though,' he pressed. 'Why wouldn't you at least consider it..?'

'I have a code,' she said, the emotion rising in her voice. 'Like, somethin' I can't break.' She stared at him. 'There are 12 rules to it. And the last one, number twelve, that's the most important.'

'What is it?'

She pronounced it slowly and deliberately. 'Shelter from life.'

'What does that even mean?'

'It means – it means that this life, 'ere, this is the one I want to have.'

'What are the other points then? Of this so-called code?'

She put her hands on her hips and adopted an 'as if I'm telling you' face.

'Come on.'

'No. It's embarrassin'. It's private, and it's embarrassin'.'

'I told you about my fuckin' death book!'

Grace let out a big laugh. 'Well,' she began reluctantly. 'Okay. Don't tell no one owt about it or yer dead meat.'

'Swear down.'

'So,' she said. 'I call it the Beggar's Code.' She cleared her throat and recited the 12 principles that were her creation. When she had finished, Gracie looked thoroughly pleased with herself.

'I'm not sure I understand what half of them mean. Or why you need a code for them.'

'Yeah. Well, that's 'cos yer brain-dead. Not my fault, is it?' She grinned and closed the book she'd been holding. 'I mean... you can talk! Like, why are you even interested in this weird shit?' She shoved it into his hands.

Red shrugged, gazing across the canal. He didn't know the answer to that himself. Just something in him, he supposed. He tried to put it into words. 'It's the thing we never talk about, death. But don't you think it's pretty important?'

'Nah. I mean, who gives a shit. It comes soon enough; I'm hardly gunna waste time wonderin' about it.'

'We don't want to even see a dead body, what death looks like. Why are we so afraid?'

'It's fuckin' ghoulish, that's why.'

'What do you think happens? When we die?'

'Nuthin'. The worms 'ave a field day. I bet a human's cheeks are like some kind of weird delicacy for a worm.'

'I don't think that.'

'Wot do you know about worms?'

'No. I mean about when we die. Life stops. But death starts. It's simply something else. Not everything that "is" has to be the same as life.'

'And now yer proper doing my nut in.' She grabbed the death book back. Flipped pages again. 'The writer probably gets off on this stuff. Has to dress it up as a science book, but really 'e's a perv. You sure you ain't a perv too?' She gave him a sideways look.

They reached a section which he had read many times. It was on the subject of child abuse: the signs that it might leave on a body, pre-mortem, post-mortem. There was a paragraph explaining that abuse sometimes had no physical signs, that abuse could be emotional and psychological, a matter of neglect as much as purposed hurt. Again, there were the pictures of the ends of lives; this time, the bodies were small, fragile and livid with punches, kicks, burns from cigarettes or hot water scalding.

Gracie lingered for a moment, then shut the book for good.

'What's up?'

'Nowt,' she said. 'I'll tell you about it one day.'

'Tell me what?'

She shook her head, and he was left to wonder. Like some dramatic unveiling, the curtains had been drawn back on the inner life of his homeless companion, only to be closed tight again. Her amber, tigress eyes shone with the startling vulnerability of a young cub.

KIN

Shane handed the small rectangular card to Martin and explained how she'd come by it.

'See the number? 334.'

'Yeah.'

'It's my best lead. Any ideas?'

'The Homeless collect things all the time.'

True. But it would have had no obvious use for Gracie. In fact, it would be hard to find a better encapsulation of muggle-like redundancy, viewed from a beggar's bleak existence, than a school library ticket. And yet she'd found it among the young woman's most treasured possessions.

'She kept it with two photos. One was of her family before everything went wrong. The other was a photo of the old man Karen told me about. The library ticket meant something to her,' she went on, a little excited. 'It stood for something.'

'It'll be the sister's then.'

'She has a photo of her.'

'People don't ration things from people they've lost, Shane. Logic doesn't apply to grief.' He paused, turning the object in his hand. 'I don't get it – it's a library card, but it doesn't say which school. There's a borrower number, handwritten, but no name.' He passed it back. 'It's like the owner doesn't want you to find them.'

Shane gave a wry smile. She felt sure it belonged to the nameless, and it was strange to imagine him pursuing anonymity in life when he was to find it so freely in death.

'I think this was a third token from her life. It belonged to the young man.'

'The nameless? Feels very tentative.'

The DAO crossed her arms. 'I want to follow it up.'

'That's why you asked for ideas.' He smirked. 'You want more time for the case.'

Shane didn't like being read. 'What's more important, a metric or doing the right thing?'

'They're not mutually exclusive.' She had seen his mouth tighten. 'You only have the word of this Karen that Gracie and the dead guy had a relationship at all.'

'Who paid for her funeral then?'

'Anyone. Some other homeless who got their life back on track. A contact from her horrendous past. Karen herself. You don't know.'

'Alan is wrong. We shouldn't be measured on this stuff. How long it takes to work out who someone was. Locating a relative to arrange a funeral. It's inhuman.'

'There has to be a cut-off point. You can't investigate forever.'

'Yeah, but you know the cut-off. From working on cases yourself. You know if a DAO is doing a decent job or not.'

'We just need to be smart about it.'

'What's happened with the redundancies?'

He shifted in his chair. 'I put the names to Alan. He reacted positively but said he has to go through his processes. It'll be before month end. I have a meeting with HR today to prepare.' His eyes travelled to the glass partition fronting his office, beyond which sat the team, including the two affected.

'Think of yourself as the messenger only.'

'It'll be fine.'

'You'll get used to it.'

'I already have. I assume you've Googled the hell out of "school library cards" and who manufactures them?'

She nodded. 'Nothing doing. I mean, there's plenty of them

on there, Amazon, eBay sellers, online stationers, but not one has a library card with this design.'

'Probably from years ago.'

'Stop being defeatist.'

His laughter broke the tension. 'Call round Manchester printing companies then. Schools don't generally buy off the high street; they use professional printers. And a lot of printers don't have a web presence; they still operate off word of mouth. I'd look at the industrial estates.'

'Good thinking. Thanks.'

'Shane,' he said as she went to leave. 'That cut-off point you talked about. The one I need to judge. On this case–'

'Yes, I know,' she said.

She worked outwards from the city centre. Consistent with Martin's advice, Shane targeted the industrial estates, seeking out printers or stationery suppliers that might have produced the mysterious card. It was a hit-and-miss method, which risked missing much of the population; after she'd been to ten estates, only four of which had printers at all, and none of them a printing contract with schools in the area, she privately acknowledged that her boss had been right in downplaying her chances.

But it only takes a tiny lead for a breakthrough to happen. As her enquiries spread further south and into the Stockport area, a small establishment recognised the card's style and finish. Not theirs, however. It belonged to a competitor.

'Printers are all different,' the man lectured in what Shane imagined was a regular lesson delivered to anyone who'd listen. 'This card isn't a high street thing, you know. Not mass produced and shipped in from China.' He rolled his eyes in disgust. 'Not our level of craftsmanship, 'course. But still. It's printed locally, and it looks like Jenner's.'

Jenner's Press was shuttered, so she looked up Companies House for the owner's full name, acquired his home address and went round. A rather wizened man opened the door. He had the sallow complexion of a long-time smoker and the receding gums of a sugary diet. His hair was flattened at the sides but sticking up on top as though he'd just got out of bed.

'I'm semi-retired,' he explained at length. 'I close a couple of days a week. Looks like one of mine,' he said, examining the card. 'Let me get my keys.'

They drove back to the workshop, and he opened up. The large presses didn't look like they'd been used for a while. There were some tools on a bench beside one of the machines.

'My wife says I should sell the business. But it's what I know. That press there,' he said, 'I had it specially imported from Hungary. These are good machines.'

'Isn't everything digital now?'

'Far from it. Some digital printers give a passable finish. But they've been developed, what, in the last ten years or so? The technology on the mechanical presses is decades old, tried and tested. You get a far better end product. Highly customisable as well. Individual.' He patted one of the presses. 'Take the card that brought you here. If that had been digitally printed, we wouldn't be having this conversation.'

There was an adjoining office. Shelving tottered with box files and ring binders. Shane saw a bulky monitor on the desk in his office; her heart sank as he moved straight past it and began pulling down binders.

'It's alright, I know exactly where everything is.'

'I'll make a cup of tea,' she said. There was a kettle on top of a filing cabinet.

'There's some powdered milk and sugar there.'

Three hours later, he still hadn't found what he was looking for. 'There's a file,' he said. 'Has all of the school contracts. Black, it is. Definitely black.'

At first, he'd been quite talkative, telling her about the 1970s, when he'd first established the business, having apprenticed out of Salford, how he'd moved premises four times. Met his wife when she came to get printing done for her father's carpet shop over in Salford. His son had joined the business on leaving school, and Jenner had planned on leaving it to him. But then he moved to Germany for a job in IT, married, settled, and that was that.

Then the old man told tales of the '80s, and suddenly Shane was in the territory of her childhood, the days of the rotary phone, of kids playing in the streets from dawn till dusk, before the ages of mobile and internet. She had witnessed the tail-end of those times when everyone knew 'a man' they could recommend to remediate all ills, from fixing white goods to pest control, and when it was word of mouth that brought custom to a Mancunian printer. The town markets were still thriving then and hotbeds of gossip exchange; she had often seen the ladies in their scarves and one good coat, carrying bags and their own high standards. Almost every man smoked and drank hard, including her father; there had been the working men's clubs, honest graft, the grand poverty.

Modernisation had a lot to answer for. It was undiscerning in what it swept away, raising living standards undeniably, but lessening community spirit. The characters were disappearing from the landscape: Lowry's Northern folk, folk that could only *be* Northern, the progeny of industry, grit and grime.

About an hour into their conversation, she had sensed the frustration bubbling up inside Jenner as his answers to questions grew shorter and his page turns snapped ever more vigorously. Shortly afterwards, they fell into complete silence. He breathed heavily, impatiently. His wife called.

'I'm at the workshop. Yes... Yes. The workshop. I can't come back at the moment. Yes. I need to finish something. Oh, about 10 minutes.'

There was no chance of him giving up his quest: it had become a personal battle to prove that his powers were untouched by time.

Shane wandered outside. The press was built on the corner of a roundabout junction, and she stood there, watching the cars swing round and away. The outskirts were so different to the city centre, with their flattened skylines and roads radiating ever outwards into the commuter belts. One of them became the Curry Mile as it encountered Rusholme in a fragrant hubbub of culture and cuisine; another led to Gorton, where Hindley and Brady had lived and murdered; and still more connected Chorlton, Sale and Wythenshawe, whose speckle of lakes and parks lined the old thoroughfares into town. It was the diverse spread of an organic conurbation, a chaos of features, like formed crystals.

Jenner appeared behind her, shuffling across the gravel. 'I've got it,' he said, the triumph in his voice.

She followed him back in.

'Was at the bottom of the filing cabinet.' It was the one she'd been making tea on. The folder was purple, not black. 'Knew it would turn up.'

There were samples for every print run he'd ever made, and this one was no different: one glance and she saw that the sample was identical to the card found in Gracie's possessions.

'This was, what, eight years ago now,' he said. 'Good card and ink, no school name, crest or graphics. Very much the basic template. Keeps the print cost down. No pre-fill, no barcoding, no laminate. The school can then complete the pupils' details by hand, you see. Makes sense as they can carry on giving them out to the new joiners without doing fresh print runs.'

'This one has a borrower reference only, number 334. No name.'

He considered. 'That'll be laziness. The borrower reference is all the school needs to fill in, long as it ties to their library lending system. Probably the students get told to add their names to the cards, but if they don't, well, the field stays blank.

I think we all know what teenagers are like.' There was the first glint of humour in the ageing face. Vindication had unlocked his spirits. 'I used to do a fair bit of business with school stationery. I can always tell the batch run, though. Printer's eye,' he said and smiled. 'Here it is,' his finger traced the name, 'order of 5,000 cards. Must have kept them going for a while. Gaskell Secondary School. Damson Road.'

Being well organised and diligent by nature, with parents who placed an emphasis on education, Shane should have done better at school. The need to apply herself had come before she was mature enough to handle it, and while she was busy denying it or introspecting on it or rebelling against the guilt, the time had simply gone. Her exam results had been mediocre, and it was the quiet disappointment of her father that had stung the most.

It felt slightly ridiculous to be dredging up these thoughts as she sat in the head teacher's office at Gaskell Secondary School, but they described days that cast long shadows into her life. She felt the discomfort that so many adults feel returning to that environment. A teacher's office retained that aura of unequal power, the memories of censure, of fear and consequence.

'I've held this position for 12 years,' said the head teacher. 'We've never reported a student missing.'

'I know,' she replied. 'I checked the missing persons database before I came.'

The head teacher eyed her, calm and cautious. 'Does Ofsted know you are here?'

'No.'

'Your note said you're from the council.'

'Yes, but not the local education authority.'

'Has a parent complained?'

'No. With your permission, I'd like to look up this reference number in your lending system.'

The head teacher considered. 'What are you looking to achieve?'

'Identification of a deceased.'

'Not a criminal investigation, though.'

Shane shook her head.

'Okay, I have no objection to that.' She unlocked her PC. 'I can access the library records from here. What's the number?'

'334.'

She pressed return. 'I recognise the name.'

'What is it?'

She clicked her mouse several times. 'Thought so. I looked in our leaver records. He transferred to another school. St Augustine's.'

'Transferred?'

'Yes.'

'What's the boy's name?'

'Red,' she said. 'Red Milliner.'

'Who told you he had moved?'

'We don't keep a record of that, but it's typically the parents. They would have provided details of the new school he was going to. Then it gets registered as such with the local education authority. You should speak with St Augustine's.'

'Do you have a photo of Red?'

It was a couple of minutes before she found what she was looking for: a school photo taken when he was 15. She turned the monitor round so that the Deceased Affairs officer could see. The boy that would later run away from everything that he knew stared back at her. She wanted to read something in his quiet eyes, but they were a barrier to interpretation: neither happy nor sad, neither innocent nor wise; he could have been any young lad of Manchester in his shirt and tie. Before he died, two homeless years would add their toll, weathering soft skin with the Street's rough touch, drawing out the pinch of cheeks and emaciated limbs, but there was no doubt that it was him. Gracie had kept Red's library card, and it had lain in the repository for a whole year waiting, so it could lead Shane here, to this face.

What might have been another bottled soul would now be freed. Whatever the iniquities of his life on Earth, and the ignominy of death, alone, with no friend to raise his name, some grace had been restored. For him. For Shane too. She had fulfilled the commitment of a graveyard, in spite of a tenuous road, the metrics, the emotion in each step. I've found you, she thought. Your name is Red, and I've found you. She could never right the wrong implanted in her particular grief, but she had righted this wrong. She had named the nameless.

In a subconscious, inquisitive movement, her hand came up, ready to touch the screen. She checked herself.

'Will you excuse me for a minute, please?'

'Of course.'

Shane found the girls' toilets and went inside. Even as she locked the cubicle door, her legs weakened, and she grasped the lid of the cistern. She closed the toilet seat and sat down. Her hand tightened into a fist, a tremble of triumph, and then it came up to her mouth, covering the broken sounds. She cried as hard as she could, purposefully, as though her soul might exit from her body, an exorcism of the unhappiness and its dominion over her. 'End!' her scream said. 'Please end.'

But it did not end.

She heard the main door to the toilets open, and a moment later, close again. She wiped her eyes and blew her nose.

On her return, the head teacher was keen to pick up where they'd left off. If Red had run away from home, she ventured, and had now lost his life in such tragic circumstances, then she was, of course, incredibly sorry. The school was always sorry to hear about anything bad happening to one of their pupils, even former pupils. And she wanted to make clear, above all, that Gaskell Secondary had followed the education authority's protocol. They had forwarded his academic record and some other standard information to the new school, and that was where their involvement had ended. He hadn't been a standout pupil; he hadn't been flagged as vulnerable or requiring dedicated support, either. Shane must agree there was nothing else they could have done to foresee or prevent the situation.

As she left the school gates, a young woman stopped her. She had been waiting by the long skirt of railings that ran along the front of the school.

'Have you come about Red?' Her hair was jet black, and her eyes were the same.

The DAO was surprised: 'Yes.'

'Word gets around when the council comes calling about a past student.'

'Are you a student?'

'Sixth form,' she said.

'Did you know Red?'

'Yes, we were friends. Is he dead?' Her voice was flat like she was inquiring about the post.

'A young man was found in the city centre; we are in the process of identifying him.'

'He was bullied, you know. Before he ran away.'

The young woman told her about the death of the homeless woman, Red being questioned by the authorities, the writing on the whiteboard, the begging bowls under his desk. The fight in the playground. Her irises stirred and glittered in the most unsettling of ways: Shane couldn't tell whether there was a bitterness to be read, complete indifference or something else entirely.

'Red wouldn't accept help. I offered to help him. But he didn't want it.' She paused. 'He was always closed off. It was who he was; he would never let anyone in.'

Perhaps he didn't trust you, Shane thought. He let Gracie in.

The teenager stared as if she was trying to read the DAO's innermost thoughts. 'Did you know him?' she asked.

'No.'

'I guess your job can't be easy. You must get involved in a case.'

Shane went to answer, but a car was coming out of the school gates, so she turned to step aside. When she looked back, the young woman was already on her way, walking back to class through a second entrance. Her raven hair danced with each step as she headed with apparent purpose.

BARE

Remarkable how a name unlocked the life of an individual, like some magic phrase that slotted into the language of records and returns and brought instantaneous meaning. Now it was easy to confirm Red's age, medical history and dental records, which might serve yet as the means of identification. Just as easy to pull the records of his parents, Terence and Bettina Milliner, and as much as the state was prepared to divulge on their documented lives.

Nothing had changed from the authorities' perspective in one notable regard: Red was still cited as living with his parents. Judging by a search of the missing persons database, his disappearance had never been reported. That suspended state of truth would now be brought to the ground by her arrival. Shane would walk up to the front door of their home and reveal that their son was dead.

Success in her job generally meant sitting opposite another human being and telling them that news. Sometimes she visualised the Named at her shoulder, witness to the recipient's reaction. Recognition of the victim's name was always instant, as was the shock of passing; whatever followed was anyone's guess. Denial, fury, grief. Fear of having to pay the funeral bill or outstanding debts. Rancour at the lost years and soured memories. Indifference sometimes, which was worst of all. In those condensed instants after her pronouncement, Shane felt as though the whole of human nature was laid out for her to observe.

The house was a standard two-up, two-down. Her eyes took in the dislodged tiles, the windowsills flaking at the corners. A lawn ripe with weeds. Pausing at the end of the path, she gathered her thoughts and rehearsed a little of what she would say.

As the bell wasn't working, and there was no knocker, she rapped with her knuckles. After three separate bouts of knocking, she finally heard footsteps, and the door opened.

Before her, stood a man in his late middle age, with one of those ratty moustaches that were long ago out of fashion and hair combed back tight to the scalp. His trousers were made of thick corduroy; he had on a blue cotton shirt and a baggy cardigan buttoned over it.

'My name is Shane Ellis. I'm from the council.'

Terence Milliner looked like a man caught with his hand in the petty cash.

'Not HMRC,' she added. 'Deceased Affairs Office.'

'Oh. Oh, right,' he said. 'Deceased.' He moved the word round his mouth like he was tasting it.

'Can I come in?'

Hesitation still showed in his footwork as though he needed to seek approval from some unknown quarter, but then he gathered himself and led the way to the living room.

The first thing Shane heard was the sound of aggressive typing and then a woman's voice saying: 'Terence. I think Premier Foods will hit a pound. We should put more in...' She stopped on seeing that her husband had not returned alone from answering the door. With half an eye on her monitor, she looked at the stranger. Then back at him.

'She's from the council. Deceased... what was it again?'

'The Deceased Affairs Office.' Shane looked at the mother. 'It's about your son, Red.'

Even from a few feet away, she saw the physical jolt at the mention of his name.

There was a long silence.

Then, almost imperceptibly, Shane observed the woman's

eye turning again, drawn once more to her screen. A low beeping noise was suddenly audible; a line graph, which refreshed constantly and was presumably the Premier Foods stock price, began to tick up. Bettina Milliner struggled to keep the panic out of her face.

'Terence. If we don't process that trade now, we'll miss the window.'

He went over, and while they collaborated on placing the order, Shane had the time to take in her surroundings and to observe a little of the woman herself.

She knew from the records that they hadn't moved house. This was where the young man had grown up. The living room was noticeably bare and neglected. There were a couple of worn sofa chairs and an old television. A sideboard lacking varnish. No pictures on the walls, no photos, nothing homely of any kind. From her position, Shane could see into the kitchen through an open door; she caught sight of dirty dishes and pot handles protruding from the sink. The sole area given love and attention was Bettina Milliner's workstation. It dominated the landscape, occupying the centre of the room where the lighting was best; the monitor and laptop formed sleek projections from its surface; reference books were stacked importantly to one side. Her chair was a padded throne.

Like a spider, the woman took care of business, fingers moving over the keyboard as articulated legs might tweak silken strands. But there was a terrible fear on show, too, in the arch of her shoulders and the hurry in her voice, of becoming a spectator at any moment to runaway share prices.

'Come on, come on,' she muttered, hammering the left button of her mouse. Her glasses were resting on her head, and she pulled them down onto her nose, then thrust them back up again. She clapped a hand over her eyes in frustration. As the ticker continued its juddery beat of ascent, she stood up and began to pace the floor. 'I put the market price, Terence. The market price, not the limit price. Why isn't it working?'

The woman stopped in profile, staring at the screen. She flicked back her hair. In Shane's mind, there was no question that Red had been Bettina's son. The area around the eyes bore the strongest similarity, from cheekbone to brow. Less clear with the father; perhaps the mouth and chin carried a likeness.

'Look, it's going through now, darling.' He rubbed her arm.

'Yes. Yes!'

Once the drama was over, the woman returned her attention to the visitor.

'I trade,' she said by way of explanation.

'Yes.'

'Equities, derivatives, FX. The markets. The pound rallied today; it's driven up a lot of stocks. Fifty bips rise for the FTSE.'

'I see.' Then she said again, 'I've come about your son, Red.'

The woman's lips drew into a tight line.

'As your husband mentioned, I work for the council. I am a Deceased Affairs officer. I get involved when, sadly, a person passes away, and we need to trace their next of kin.' Through long practice, Shane paused, allowing time for the information to be processed. 'A young man passed away in Manchester city centre, and we have reason to believe it might be Red.'

'He left,' she said. 'We don't know where he is.'

'Do you have a photograph of him?' asked Shane.

'Yes.' It was the father who spoke. He went over to the sideboard and rummaged in its drawers.

Out of the corner of her eye, Shane saw the mother's head turning back to her screen as if drawn on a string.

He exhausted each drawer and came back empty-handed. 'It may be upstairs.'

His remark was wasted on his wife, who had revolved entirely in her chair now, neck craning toward the screen, hand on mouse, shoulders hunched again.

Despite all the experience that Shane had acquired over the years, encountering the strange, discomforting situations that orbited the Nameless, she still couldn't bear to sit there, waiting, while the clicks broke obstinately upon the silence. She rose from her seat and followed Terence Milliner upstairs.

From one of the rooms came the squeak of drawers opening and closing and the rustle of papers; the door was ajar, and the DAO could see, reflected in a mirror, a woman's coat folded over the back of a chair. If that was the room they shared, then the other bedroom must have belonged to the boy. Curiosity drove her on. She stepped across the landing and opened the door to the second room.

It was empty. Not just empty. Bare. Like it had been stripped. No sign of a young man's possessions, no bed that he'd slept in, no curtains that he'd opened in the morning and closed at night. No carpet, only floorboards. The disposal of all their child's belongings could have been mistaken for a spiteful response to abandonment or the fraught psychology of moving on, but no, Shane thought, this was a utilitarian decision. The paltry proceeds would have been invested into Premier Foods or another equity of choice.

She walked to the window and looked out, taking in the lonely view, the well-ordered rows of houses and the back gardens with their scooters, footballs and plastic furniture. Her hand rested on the windowsill, then momentarily on the glass itself, as she contemplated Red's past occupancy of this humble space, his seat of suffering. His home had not been the site of terrible degradation, of violent action, the type that had scarred Gracie's life and seen her sister killed. But it had been a scene of harm, nonetheless. Abuse was not just a matter of fists and neglect. Not solely malnutrition. Addiction took other shapes than the point of a needle. His parents had a habit which meant that this had never been a home.

As Shane shut the door, she realised the man was at her shoulder. She turned and met his gaze. There was no anger at her unwarranted intrusion, but neither did he demand an explanation. His eyes had a powerless look to them as though he'd long ago become a passenger to life's events. He opened his mouth, but a shriek downstairs grabbed their attention.

Delight shone in Bettina's eyes when they descended, which she quickly checked on seeing Shane. A glance at the monitor revealed a dramatic uptick in the stock tracker.

'This is a school photo,' the man said, holding it out to the DAO.

It was the same as the one she had been shown by Gaskell's head teacher. How, in the age of the smartphone, could this be the only photo available?

'Is it him?' he asked.

'I believe so. I'm very sorry. As part of our process, a visual identification will need to be completed.'

'What does that mean?' It was the mother. Shane noticed that her fingers had started to fidget.

'One of you will need to see Red. To identify him, formally.'

'I... I can't. How long will that take?'

'I can do it,' Terence said.

'Following identification, his body will be released. For funeral arrangements to be made.'

'We won't be able to pay for it.'

Shane's mouth fell open. In retrospect, there was an inevitability to it, but the comment had caught her off guard.

The woman refused to look at her. 'We can't. He made his decision. *He* left *us*. He abandoned us! After everything we'd done for him. Even if it is him. What if it's not him? It's probably not him. It could be anyone!'

'It's your son,' said Shane.

'This is too much,' she said, 'it is simply too much.' She

crossed her arms and shook her head. 'Who are you? To say it's our son.'

A volcanic fury, quite unlike anything she'd felt for a long, long time, took possession of Shane. 'He *was* your son!' Her hands were up and waving. The words were caught in her throat. 'He was your *son!*'

'You can't speak to us like this.'

The woman had folded her arms. She wore a crazed smile.

'He was never reported as missing,' Shane finally managed to blurt out, the accusation naked in her voice. 'You told his school that he had moved to another school. You should never have been his parents. You don't deserve to be parents!'

Shane clenched and unclenched her hands, all her helplessness gathering in her fingertips. She felt as though she would explode. They'd had the very chance she craved, and they'd chucked it away. She would tear down the walls of this unbearable home, smash the computer with its terrible ticker, turn over the table and that throne.

'Get out!' Bettina Milliner screamed. 'Get out!'

STEEL

'I received a complaint about you.'

Shane could feel the eyes of the rest of the team through the glass panelling to Martin's office.

'I can't do this here,' she said. 'Can we go for a coffee? Discuss it there.'

'I have a report to produce by four.'

She shifted in her seat. 'They wouldn't pay for the funeral.'

'And?'

'After all that. We find out his identity, and then they can't even be bothered to claim their son. It–'

'I had a call from the school as well, the one he went to.' The gaze of her former peer had settled on a spot somewhere above her head. 'Something about strange behaviours. Implying the school hadn't done what it needed to. Crying in the girl's toilets.'

Shane was stunned.

'This case is at an end. Complete the identification. If the Milliners will do it, fine. Otherwise, use dental records. You need to move on from it.'

'They're his parents, Martin. I do not understand.'

'It's not your concern. We do our job. We can't force anyone to bury their dead – you know that as well as I do.' Now his eyes met hers. 'None of this is new. We've both been doing this job for 10 years.'

'This is different.'

'How?'

She wanted to tell him how it was different from all her other cases, about the commitment she'd made to the young man, and in some proximate way, to her ectopic. She wanted to talk about the sacrifice Red had undergone for Gracie to ensure her life had been marked in the right way upon its ending. She wanted to say that now that the nameless was named, the neglect he had suffered in life must not be replicated in death.

'Why did you do the job for ten years?' She challenged.

'What do you mean?'

'You said I had pretty much no chance of even getting his name. And now I'm being criticised for following up. I can't win!'

'The point is that it's time to move on. The dead bodies don't stop arriving. And I had a cut of the metrics yesterday,' he said, the concern showing on his face. 'We're not on track. I need my best people – namely you – getting through more cases. You can't stick on one.'

'They didn't even report him missing, did you know that? They said he was going to another school. Isn't that a crime? Misleading the authorities about where your child is?'

'If you feel that strongly, pass it to the police to look at.'

'They will do nothing, and you know it.'

'Our involvement ends here, Shane. Now.'

One by one, she switched on the lights in the hallway, living room and kitchen. She could not sleep. Ryan would sleep through. The kettle gave out its prompt, incipient hum, but a moment later, she switched it off again. The Deceased Affairs officer leaned on the countertop and looked up, catching sight of her face in the window, framed by the black of night. It was a face contorted with pain and unquenchable anger.

So, he would have a pauper's burial after all. She might well have found his name, but she had not found parents ready to pay for the finalities of the boy christened Red Milliner. She refused to believe that they could not. They had the money. Could find the money. It was simply a continuation in death of how they had been towards him in life. Their crime was self-absorbed indifference. The son they cherished was made not of flesh and bone but of digits and symbols, and his name was the FTSE 100.

At his moment of greatest need, they had no doubt been utterly absent too. Parents who didn't give a shit about a child in the first place were unlikely to care when he stumbled upon a dead homeless woman and was interviewed by the police. They would have had no appetite to understand his fear and anxiety; the bullying of his classmates would have been a burden he shouldered alone; the ordeal could only have reinforced how little he mattered to anyone. Small wonder that he'd wanted to escape it all.

It was terrible to contemplate the road that he had taken: packing his bags and taking to the Street, having just witnessed the outcome of that journey in a beggar's lonely corpse. Had he stepped mentally into those tattered shoes? Had he foreseen the same desperate odyssey for himself? It lent a fatalistic quality to those last years of his life, a knowingness, even intentionality, to the tragedy of an early ending.

The old pain lurched in her chest. What was she trying to achieve? Change people who couldn't care less? Be some kind of social reformer? Make Red's story never repeat, when it was happening 24/7 all over the city and its sprawling suburbs. Stupid Shane. Stupid, stupid Shane. Your powerlessness to save those lives is no different from your powerlessness to save the life that was inside you.

On the kitchen worktop, a knife block pointed its handles in her direction. She drew out the largest of the knives, spread her hand on the chopping board and positioned the blade across her thumb. Karen had said the young man seemed better after the removal of his thumb, like his heartbreak had been salved. An external loss to replace the internal one. A visual reminder to keep the mind from turning.

Red had paid for Gracie's funeral. There was little doubt in Shane's mind. But a burial cost a thousand pounds, even with the plainest headstone, the cheapest casket, and the most perfunctory of ceremonies. It could be two or three times that. How could a homeless man, begging on the street or even odd-jobbing for cash, have that kind of money?

He must have borrowed it from loansharks, the street-lenders who ordinarily preyed on addicts gasping for their next fix, knowing full well that he would never be able to pay them back. And then? They had exacted the penalty with a sharp instrument. He had given his thumb to regain control of his grief, and in the language of exchange, of something tangible for something intangible, it was a trade that made sense to Shane.

The steel shone. One quick stroke? A slow, surgical slice of the flesh? You had to get right through the bone. Only severance would do. A block of heavy wood, perhaps, hammered down on the blade. She would need a ligature to stem the blood. She would visualise all of her pain channelled into that single thumb, tie it off, and cut away that appendage of suffering.

After a long, pregnant silence, she rested the cold flat blade on the back of her hand. Then returned it to the block.

What would her ectopic think of the matter?

The first hints of dawn were coming. Her eyes were drawn to the window, to the beginnings of that day's tender light, and she could imagine the little bud of life, held in stasis, hovering somewhere there, at the cusp of promise – promising the baby, the child, the adult, it would never become. The image of a bee came to her again, the exquisite Mancunian bee, and then some strange equating of the two, the bee and her ectopic: a metamorphosis. Unexpected comfort lay in those simple lines: the folded wings, the tiny, furred body. The bee was curled up as though preserving its potential, as though the image itself could come alive. There was no mouth to speak, but there was a presence, and a voice, some telepathic launch of thought. Shane's powerlessness altered at that moment, undergoing its own metamorphosis. It transitioned into a sudden thoughtfulness, an impetuous surge.

An idea.

GHOST

Darren left their company as abruptly as he'd arrived. One minute he seemed to be forever turning up, making Gracie laugh at terribly unfunny things or dropping sarcastic comments in Red's direction; the next minute, it was as if he'd never existed. Perhaps he'd vacated Manchester entirely, but it hardly mattered. Red was just glad that he no longer had to set eyes on that overconfident expression, the ridiculous bulldog walk and his permanently brandished tattoo.

Then one day Bart confided, 'You remember how I said I'd speak with him, tell him he wasn't wanted around here? Well, dear boy, I more than took my chance.'

'Really?'

'Yes.' The eyes smiled, and in that instant, the man looked rejuvenated. Red caught himself imagining what Bartholomew had looked like as a younger man, his hair a sandy brown before time turned it white. Arriving in China, perhaps, unaware that he would spend half his life there.

'What did he say?'

'Not a great deal. Simply walked off. Good riddance, as far as I'm concerned.'

Bart was so sure of himself and so ecstatic at dishing it out to the other man that Red said nothing further. A disquiet lingered though. The old man was normally so measured and wise; he did not sound like himself. It was as though the perceived threat to Gracie had made him foolhardy. Nor did it sound like Darren to walk away without contriving some response or retaliation. Even the shortest conversation showed that he needed to come out on top in any given situation.

Curiosity got the better of Red after a few days.

'So why did he leave?'

'It's private.' Gracie was mending Bartholomew's jacket as she spoke and did not look up.

The young man sat on the ground, his arms round his knees, gazing out over the canal.

She flicked her hair over one shoulder and pulled sharply on a thread. She bit the end off between her teeth. 'He said I didn't need 'im no more.'

'What does that mean?'

'Wot it says.'

'And do you need him?'

'I dunno.' She paused. 'Truth is. I don't need no one.'

The Street had a way of eroding the near past in that she respected solely the present, and it didn't take long for Red to forget about Darren, and for the most part, Noura too. With no watches to check or schedules to follow, time lost its instancy, returning to a shape the ancients must have known, where sunrise and sunset were all that caught the eye, and the rest was a gradually shifting light. A lack of purpose added to the haze: there were no lessons for Red to attend, no predetermined lunch times, no need to sleep or rise at particular hours. Stepping away from the muggle clock was a form of deliverance, but it could also be jarring to glimpse the date on a discarded newspaper and discover that days, weeks, occasionally months had rushed by without realising.

Meanwhile, the beggar boy had changed and grown. He had begun to grasp the true meaning of homeless life. The superficial definition of being home-less by name was a world away from the actuality of all that it proved to be. Vagabond existence crept up on you over many months, effecting change in fundamental ways: the way you moved, the way you ate, the way you smelled. Above all, the way you thought. Your mind was centred on the here and now, the upcoming meal, a safe passage through to the day's end. There was scant thought given to the future, to dreams and prospects, to hopes or visions.

The Street was changing too. The shelters appeared more crowded than they'd ever known, and the competitive element, from queuing for food to securing a temporary bed, was on full display. They witnessed, at a distance, the thump of fists and panicked wrestling over a last place; they heard one rough sleeper bragging to another that his needs were greater and threatening brute force as persuasion. An increase in numbers was matched by a broadening of type: a whole spectrum of muggles, fallen foul of unemployment and rising rents and unfamiliar with hardship, were ending up newly on the streets.

Then Spice arrived. Once again, Bart was first to preach the dangers, forewarning them to steer clear of that particular drug at all costs. It was circulating widely, was cheap and incredibly addictive. Soon afterwards, they began to witness with alarming frequency the effects which were its hallmark: the dread catalepsy, the bowed petrifaction of addicts, their eyes fixed somewhere between rapture and stupor. Most of them were rough sleepers, and some of them they knew. Their dignity was abandoned outside shop fronts, on benches or by the rubbish bins of Piccadilly Gardens.

The rumours of someone having it in for the Homeless had not abated. The terror had intensified; the attacker was 'out of control'. They had become somewhat of a bogeyman – the malevolent hand behind every blow, cut and kick suffered by a streetsleeper. They operated in darkness, preying on the solitary, slitting a face here, removing an ear there. There was always a ton of blood and a lasting token to remember. It was possible there was more than one assailant, but descriptions suggested it was down to a single hater of the community. Although such violence was hardly unusual, this appeared purposeful and premeditated in a way which was rarer. Their objective was not to kill; it was to maim and disfigure.

'It's all overplayed,' Gracie said. 'Some fuckin' doosh. Probably drunken brawls.'

Red had spoken with Bart and raised the question of arming themselves for protection. 'I carry two weapons, my dear chap. Cunning and guile. Oh, and if all else fails, erudition. I like to educate an assailant out of their mischief.'

'Hm. And what if they don't want to learn?'

On the night he came across the attacker, Red was walking away from the Gardens, having finished an evening begging on his own, as Gracie had gone off to see her Brazilian friend, Adriana, who'd finally been placed in accommodation.

He was on a well-lit street in the Northern Quarter. As he passed one of the arts and crafts shops, his eye caught the flicker of his reflection in the large plate glass window. He retraced his steps. It was a while since he'd looked in a full-length mirror. The sudden presentation of his gaunt face and lank hair and budding facial growth took him by surprise. Not only did he feel homeless now, he looked it too. One eyelid was swollen, and he had no idea why. His fingers were bloated from the cold and the damp. All this despite his best efforts to remain clean and nourished and to retain some of the dignity with which Gracie lived her life.

It was so hard. Physical changes influenced psychological ones and vice versa. Three square meals a day were impossible to achieve; your trousers became loose as your waist and stomach shrank; your hunger shrank with them. It was a circle of diminution. Perversely, you ended up forcing yourself to eat. But then, at other times, in an abrupt wilfulness, your brain developed an overpowering lust for food – perhaps after aromas escaped from a nearby bakery. Rough brown crust. Soft, white crumb. Thick yellow butter.

He reached to touch his pale face. There were moments like this when the shape he cast was so undernourished and negligible that he could have been weightless or within a hair's breadth of non-existence. He didn't mean death by that. Very specifically, non-existence, a lack of physical presence, like some ghost of the streets, a phantom without dimension. It was then that he could understand that it was possible to pass through the world and leave no trace at all; in his darkest moments, he could imagine vanishing in an instant with no one even noticing.

Would the people from his first life recognise this ghost? Joe, Dan, Melanie, his mother, his father? If he stood before them now, would they embrace him, be too stunned for words or shrug with a terrible indifference?

Pick yourself up, he told himself. Self-pity was a pointless refuge. He was alive, swollen eye or not, and that was all that mattered. Look around you! he thought. This is your kingdom. He smirked at his foolishness, recalling his conversations with Noura. Kingdom? Are you serious? Yes! It may not be much, but everything here, in this life, is a decision you have made. A rejection of the misery you were in. It may not be glossy or glamorous, but no one dictates who you are or what you may become.

He emphasised each word again, watching his lips move in the glass. Pick. Yourself. Up. As he did so, his eyes were drawn to another movement in the mirrored light.

There were two figures. Even in the reflection, Red detected something unusual: a discordance in their silhouettes, an aberrant, stilted motion. Turning, he observed how they stood as adversaries, feet planted and arms primed, down the alleyway opposite. Instantly he saw that one of them was Gracie.

Surely Gracie was with Adriana.

Then his heart thundered as he saw a gleam in the protagonist's hand, and the thought of violence and mania, of stabbing and defiling, perpetrated on the Homeless by some unnamed force for evil, burst upon his mind.

'Gracie!' he began. His voice failed.

From under the safe, stark light of the main street, he bolted forwards, motivated by fear, heading for the darker ground.

They had shifted, crabbing in a circle, and Red could see that the young woman would soon be trapped in the shuttered doorway to a building. He hesitated, on the cusp of bystanding. He was no more skilled in fighting now than he had been in the playground brawl all that time ago.

But he could not abandon his companion.

Now they had rotated so that the assailant's back faced him; it was his chance. As he dashed forward, he saw Gracie's eyes and the lustre of terror, shock and relief, all combined. He punched, he kicked, and before he had breathed again, the furious shadow was revolving into him. But Red was too close for the weapon to reach, and instead, he felt the brunt of the man's elbow, just above his swollen eye.

The figure was tall, young. Not deranged but calmly furious, as though determined to right a transparent wrong.

'Fucking homeless cunt. I'm going to cut you.'

The arm holding the knife was held a little lower, ready to impart full force.

Red sensed Gracie moving beside him.

'Run!' she screamed.

Of all the times to think of Melanie, this was probably the worst. Blood was coming down his face and into his mouth; she entered his thoughts with the same bitter taste. He remembered her smirk during that playground fight, when he was at his most vulnerable, and found that it had the power to galvanise him.

'You may be a shark, but I am a fucking WOLF.' He roared at

the top of his lungs. Madly, he threw himself on the man, dodging a thrust of the knife. The momentum pulled at them, gyrating and tilting. The attacker's head struck the solid, Mancunian brick of one of the buildings lining the alley.

He could not have been much older than Red. Dead to the world, breathing gently, he lay on the tarmac like an innocent, his motivations completely unknown, the foul words a mystery. Seen properly under lamplight, it was an ordinary muggle face, no hint of malevolence in rest.

'Stand back,' said Gracie.

The knife was lying harmlessly across the attacker's uncurled fingers, and she picked it up.

'What are you doing?'

''E needs a lesson.'

Red grabbed her arm, but she shook herself free.

'I'm gunna give him summat to remember us – and every other 'omeless – by.'

'But–'

'No.' She stared at Red with a determination he'd never seen before. 'It's only right.'

She crouched and brought the blade to the unconscious figure's cheekbone. Blood began to well where she pressed it. She drew the tip down with energy along the cheek and jawline. Red saw the skin ripple and burst. The flesh underneath. A glimpse of bone.

'Let's go.'

'We can't leave him. What if he bleeds to death?'

Gracie started to walk away.

Red spotted a group of passersby on the main street. Shame they hadn't been there earlier.

'Hey!' he shouted, waving. 'Hey! Call an ambulance!' He waved again. Finally, one turned. 'Dial 999! He needs an ambulance!'

Then the two beggars turned on their heels and fled.

GEMINI

Back at the canal, Bart received a breathless account of what had gone down. The only element neglected was how Gracie had given the assailant a taste of his own medicine: a detail not withheld as such but not volunteered either. After the telling was done, the old man embraced her; she returned the hug, and then, resistant as ever to sentimentality, brushed him off.

'I'm fine. Let's not make a drama out of it.'

Bart clapped the young man on the shoulder and thanked him.

'It was nothing,' he said. 'Anyone would have done the same.'

Inside, though, his soul glittered with pride. Looking back over the years he'd spent in the suburban solitude of Heaton Moor and these metamorphic months as a 'bond of the city centre, it was probably the single bravest thing he'd ever done. The one truly useful thing. A thing which others could praise.

In her hour of need, he had been there for Gracie. Finally, he had repaid the first-day debt that he owed her, and in that moment, when he had seen her fear laid bare, chased by the rallying hope of his appearance, he had known the exhilaration of being needed by another human being. And, perhaps, of needing one too.

Later that night, once the old man was asleep, Red said to Gracie: 'I don't know, it's just the violence of it. Violence doesn't solve anything, does it?'

'He 'ad it comin'.'

'Do we even know it was him, though? The one who's been doing it to us homeless?'

'Well, he weren't in that alley looking for lost change, were he?'

'I guess. But he could have been a random mugger.'

'Weren't it enough for yer that he called yer a "fucking homeless cunt"? That 'e was gunna slice yer from ear to ear? 'Course it were him. Besides, you missed out on our pleasant little chat before you arrived. He jumped me. Fuckin' psycho. Started ranting 'bout the Homeless gettin' what's coming to them and 'ow he'd cut me a new arsehole. Knew a lot o' big words, that lad. Nob.'

'Why weren't you with Adriana?'

'Well, I were. But then she had to go, somethin' about meeting a housing officer. Good luck to 'er, I say. It's wot she wants.'

'Do you think he's going to hate us less, though? After that? No! He'll hate the Homeless more, Gracie. Every time he looks in the mirror.'

'So wot? It'll make 'im think twice about doin' it. Eye for an eye. In fact, he's lucky I didn't take 'is eyes. Slashing people up. I mean, how dare he? Who the fuck does 'e think 'e is?'

They were quiet for a minute, thinking.

She chuckled. 'Wot was that bit you shouted before yer went for 'im? "You're a shark. But I'm a wolf!"' Her eyes shone with delight. 'One of the funniest things I've ever heard in me life!'

'Well,' Red said, a little embarrassed, 'I was thinking of that thing you said. From your "code". "A shark is a wolf is a shark". Or whatever it is.' He rolled his eyes.

'If we don't look after our own, who will? If yer looking for justice, yer can forget the fuckin' gimps, I tell yer that.'

'I wasn't thinking of the "fucking gimps",' he said. They'd lit a fire in a can, and he poked at it, stick in hand. 'I wouldn't be going to them. Believe you me.' If anyone was entitled to complain about his experiences with the police, it was him. 'I was arrested once, you know.'

'Huh? Thought you was Mr Squeaky Clean.'

'Well, taken in for "voluntary" questioning. Was before I ran away. One morning, when I was walking to school, there was a body, just lying there–'

'A body?'

'Yeah. Down this lane connecting two of the streets. One of those little passageways that terraced houses back onto.'

'They call 'em ginnels.'

'It was a homeless woman. She was stretched out. From a distance, she looked quite peaceful, but then close up, things were different. Her face was bruised and swollen like she'd been punched or maybe kicked. I'd never seen a dead body before.' He lifted his gaze from the fire and looked at Gracie. 'Except in that book I showed you. The one I found in the school library. So I dunno, I wanted to look at her for a moment.'

'Said you was a perv.'

'Be serious for once!'

'Sorry.'

'I know it sounds weird. But it was to see what it was like. Death. To look it in the eye.'

'And?'

'It was like she'd gone. But not.'

'Huh.'

'The cells in the body die at different rates, did you know that? Some of that woman, as I stood and looked at her, some of her was still alive.'

He had committed to memory page 37 of the book on pathology, which was a step-by-step description of the process of death. Blood pressure falls, circulation stops, reflexes are lost, the metabolic reserves in individual cells begin to dissipate, neurons may fire and twitch, fluids may leak. It takes hours, days sometimes. That grey, protracted border between life and death gave a sense of graduated progression that could almost mean continuation or, at least, a smooth transition from animation to stillness. There was no abrupt rupture, no precision of expiration. And it had left him wondering whether death – in any concrete, specified moment that you could point to and hold up – ever happened at all. When he'd looked at the homeless woman, stretched out on the floor, at which point in that process had she been? In her calm, quiet form, he'd seen no jagged truths, only repose, a rightful return perhaps for a body that had cycled and the harmonised continuity of the living and the dead.

'And when the very last cell dies?'

'Maybe something else has already begun. If something looks dead but isn't, where do things truly end, and where do they begin?'

'Nah, mate. A dead body is just that – dead. It's obvious.'

'The police questioned me. They were so suspicious. Some guy from the neighbourhood saw me standing over her. I lied to them. I told them I didn't touch her. But I did, Gracie. For a split second. I touched her hand. I wanted to see how cold it was. Whether it felt alive.'

'And did it?'

'It felt like the hand of a homeless,' he said. 'No sign of Nivea.' Gently he rubbed his hands together against the chill air. 'What about you? Ever been in trouble with the law?'

She nodded curtly, and once again, he sensed he was treading into the territory of a troubled early life, the details of which she was unwilling to share. He wondered whether she would ever be ready, as Bart had said, to initiate him into what had happened.

'Yer eye's bleeding again. It needs cleaning.'

Gracie took the rag with clean, warm water and rubbed it carefully over his brow. She took his hand and put the cloth in it. He held it against his head until the bleeding stopped. This was again the different Gracie, her alter-ego, the other half of the Gemini, glimpsed in moments: tender, motherly, the way she was with Bart whenever he was in need.

Few days ever went by without Red thinking back to his first meeting with Gracie. While he might remember in great detail how the guy Marek had almost lured him into unnamed horrors, he still had no insight into why Gracie had fiercely intervened. She had put herself at risk. It bothered him that he didn't know the reason.

Now he asked.

She brushed it off with her usual whirlwind of words and temper.

'You looked fuckin' clueless, that's why.'

Then she surprised him. With her back still turned, she added: 'I dunno. You looked like you were a good person. You 'ad a kind face. That was all.' A pause. 'That and me being a mug.'

'Oh, cheers.'

'There's summat I never told yer,' she said. 'The wallet, yer money, when you were first on the Street?'

'You stole it?'

'No! 'Course I didn't! But I found it – empty like. Some sod had lifted the potato and chucked it down the towpath. I said nowt though. You wouldn't have believed me anyhow!'

'Why are you telling me this?'

'Dunno. Were getting weird you didn't know.'

Red smiled.

'I've kept it. Wan' it back?'

He considered for a moment. 'No.'

'There were a piece o' card in it.' She laughed. 'Thief didn't want that.'

Red frowned, as if remembering. 'My library card. From school.' He'd abandoned almost everything when he left home. That had come with him, though, as if he still intended to return the pathology book and borrow it legitimately, one day.

'Why did you keep it?' he asked. 'The wallet?'

'Waste not want not.' Gracie paused. 'Thanks, by the way.'

'It's just a wallet.'

'No... For being a wolf, when I was being attacked by a shark.'

'Second time I've saved you.'

'Big 'ead.'

THE GIMPS

Not long after, Red had another encounter with the police.

Following the attack, the young man was cautious about unpopulated areas, particularly if he were alone, and had decided that each of them should obtain a weapon. The punishment that Gracie had exacted on the assailant troubled him deeply. He saw the figure's hate-filled shape in the shadowy gullies that grew between buildings when evening came; he heard the tread of sickly vengeful feet in the dead of sleep. With a face scarred for life, the attacker might never venture onto the streets; equally, he might be out there every night, awaiting his moment.

They would buy three kitchen knives and carry them at all times: small blades with light handles that could be hidden down a sock or in a pocket. Gracie protested that they'd taught the guy a lesson he would never forget, that there was no need to be 'tooled up', but Red insisted. It had taken some days to beg their way to the funds that they needed, and they were now ready to window shop.

The three of them were walking through the city centre, Bart looking a touch more dishevelled than the others, and had just reached the intersection of Portland Street and Piccadilly when a young man came tearing out of a phone shop some 10 yards ahead of them. He had quite a turn of pace, his jacket billowing as it caught the wind, and he'd scampered round the corner before the shop owner had stumbled out of the door. A PCSO in the Gardens noticed the commotion and came briskly over, speaking into her radio for support. A man in his late 50s, completely unconnected to the whole incident, pointed at Red and said, 'It was him what did it,' as he walked past.

'Fuckin' muggle,' Gracie muttered under her breath.

Red raised his hands in protested innocence. But it was too late. Attention had shifted to him, and instead of chasing the real miscreant, the PCSO pulled him and his companions to one side.

The shopkeeper was breathing heavily, probably more from adrenaline than physical exertion, and he just managed to say, 'I... I'm not sure. I... no, I don't think it was him. Oh, I don't know.' Which, of course, was no help at all.

Other police arrived. One copper, who was bigger than the rest and with an appetite for taking charge of situations, asked Red if he could have a word. They stepped under the awning of the shop, out of the way of bystanders, many of whom goggled at the unfolding scene. Gracie and Bart stuck to their friend like glue.

''E's never even been into that shop,' said Gracie, and Red could hear the protective anger in her voice, only inches from the surface. The young man had been struck dumb; the old fear, borne of those hours he'd spent in police custody, answering terrible questions about a death he had nothing to do with, had come rushing back. 'It's 'cos he's 'omeless, innit?' Gracie's voice came again, and Red was dimly aware of Bart trying to calm her down.

'What's your name?'

'We don't 'ave to give no names.'

'My question was not directed at you.' He glared, then turned back to the boy. 'What's your name, son?'

'We don't 'ave to give no names. We don't 'ave to give yer owt,' Gracie said again. 'He didn't do nowt.' She grabbed her companion by the arm. 'You don't 'ave to give him yer name.'

'Yes, you do.'

'Says who? There's no law. No law sayin' we do.'

'If I give you a fixed penalty notice, you do. Then, if you don't give your name, I can arrest you.'

Red finally found his voice. He wasn't about to get arrested. 'Let's calm down for a moment. My name is R–'

'Don't gi' him yer fucking name!' She pounced on him. 'Wot you givin' a fixed penalty notice for, hey? We ain't done nuthin', *Cunt*stable.'

The copper had heard it all before and knew the power lay entirely with him. The lippy ginger girl, with her ropey knowledge of the law, short-ass physique and ragtag, indigent sidekicks, looked about as far from an instigator of civil rebellion as you could imagine. He might almost have been amused by the naked disparity in the fight.

'PSPO,' he said. 'Public space protection order. For begging and loitering with intent. This is a public space. You're disturbing it.' He glanced at the nearby police van, a clear indication to all present that he could bundle them in there if there was any more trouble.

Gracie was unmoved. 'So – nuthin' to do wi' this ridiculous theft yer accusing him of. And wot evidence d'yer 'ave that we've been disturbin' people?' She suddenly lunged at a random onlooker. 'Oi, mate. Oi – yes, you.' The onlooker quickly veered off in another direction. 'Am I disturbing you? Am I? See?' She turned back to the police officer. 'There yer go. Not disturbin' 'im at all.'

Bartholomew, who had been quiet all this time, sensed the opportunity to intervene.

'Officer, if I may take a moment of your time, please. As you may be aware, the Home Office recently issued guidance to councils directing them not to target homeless people in matters of public order, given their challenging circumstances. In respect of those challenges, the publication noted that 74% of all local authorities are unable to find suitable accommodation for those sleeping rough, following an 83% increase in homelessness on the streets of Britain in the last four years.'

Red could see the police officer evaluating this different proposition: the earnest, white-bearded face, the jumble of unkempt clothes, the articulacy and the risk posed by someone who had sharp faculties and was well-informed.

'I see, sir.'

'Indeed,' the tramp pursued, 'there was a case subject to court proceedings last month in the local authority of Haringey, where the vagrant had his breach of PSPO conviction overturned on appeal, as, in the words of the judge, "this was merely punishing the individual for being destitute".' He barely paused for breath. The shopkeeper was still standing alongside and looked like he might rub his eyes to check what he was witnessing. 'Over 300,000 people now live on the streets of Britain. In the Greater Manchester area alone, 1 in 100 of the population is homeless, and those individuals all look to the likes of your good self, officer, in this epidemic of destitution, for protection and care. These were figures quoted in an edition of The Manchester Evening News last week.'

'Understood, sir. But those statistics won't prevent me doing the job that I am employed to do.'

'Agreed, officer, but unfortunately, you have the wrong man. The true offender ran that way, down Lever Street. He was wearing a navy blue bomber jacket, black denim jeans and trainers. They were Nike, grey upper, white midsole. And he wore a basketball cap, black.'

'I see.' There was a definite change in the police officer's eagerness to press on with his questioning. He wandered a little away from them and consorted with his colleagues; a pair of them drove off. A few minutes later, he answered his radio. He listened and spoke a couple of times.

Not easily given to good grace, even in defeat, the copper looked solely at Bart and gave a terse nod. Without a further word, he went with the shopkeeper back into his shop, and the three were left with their freedom.

'Fucking gimps,' Gracie called after him. 'Haven't yer got a

Maccy D's to be getting to?'

Grabbing an arm each, Red and Bart hurried the young woman down the street and away.

'Why did yer butt in?' she badgered the old man once they were out of harm's reach. 'I 'ad it covered.'

'Are you joking?' Red scoffed. 'He saved our bacon! You almost got us arrested. This man here,' he patted the gently stooping back, 'is the one who got us out of it.'

'We left with our tails between our legs!'

'Better than losing our tails!'

They turned down Corporation Street and reached Exchange Square. There was amphitheatre-style seating, and they sat together on the cold, stone arcs, looking down towards the Old Shambles and Sinclair's Oyster Bar, which sheltered in the lee of the cathedral.

Half-timbered in the monochrome Tudor style, the Shambles had originated in the 1500s and was the oldest public house in Manchester. It had withstood all manner of generational decline and civic uplift, the Blitz bombing raids and a complete structural relocation following the IRA bomb.

Nearby was the Arndale, child of the '70s, Manchester's retail hub, where a drone of activity went on. Northern folk milled around, bustling their way up the steps and into its heart, minding their muggle business and indifferent to the three figures observing them from their detached vantage point. They really weren't disturbing anyone, Red thought, and a tiny smile broke upon his lips.

'How did you come up with all that stuff, Bart?'

'Ah, an old skill.'

'Impressive remembering all that...'

The man laughed. 'No, I mean the art of blagging. A small concoction. A mild embroidering. I'm sure the figures sounded very convincing. But most importantly, he had no way to disprove them.'

'You made them up?'

'Naturally.'

Gracie said, 'That's typical B, that is.'

'It wasn't truly about the numbers. The sentiment was enough. Besides, our bobby-on-the-beat didn't genuinely *want* to arrest us. It was a performance for the public. He needed a face-saving exit, and I supplied it.'

Red looked dubious. He caught Gracie and the old man glancing at each other and sensed a telepathy going on.

'It's time, my dear boy, that we enlightened you.'

'Huh?'

'About how things really work.'

ANGEL OF MANCHESTER

'It's rather a dirty secret,' said the old man. 'But one that you should hear.'

Red was sat in the middle; Bart and Gracie adjusted their positions inwards, and he was suddenly the child being educated by solicitous parents.

'Put aside for a minute what you think you know. About the role of the Homeless in society.'

'Role?'

'In spite of what they say, the authorities don't genuinely want people like ourselves off the Street. It's a perfect system,' Bart said, the sincerity visible on his face, 'for them and for all involved. What better way to keep the Muggles in check – docile, obedient – than the glorious illustration in their city centres of what happens when an orderly life goes wrong? There but for the grace of God go I! thinks every muggle as they walk past our kind. They're held wonderfully in fear at how precarious their lives are – if they don't have that meaningless job that pays the monthly mortgage and all those little taxes and every single bill...'

Red scoffed. 'Sounds like a conspiracy theory to me.'

'Well, you're an intelligent fellow. You can make up your own mind. But one thing is for certain. If, when people became homeless, the councils efficiently supported them back to permanent housing, there would be uproar.'

'How do you mean?'

'The Muggles desire our suffering.'

'I don't agree with that.'

'My dear boy, it is the natural order. People need to see a beggar having it hard to reinforce the notion that our life is a life apart. And one which they don't want to lead. The Muggles don't want it easy for us. Why would they? They're living these awful, pinned-down lives.'

'Slaves in the matrix,' said Gracie.

'They approve of charity but not *charity*. There's no such thing as a free lunch. That's not malice on their part. That's human nature!'

'Not true,' said Red. 'If you're a muggle, you don't want us on the streets, lurking on corners, begging for money.'

'So they would prefer us living next door?'

'Yes. No. Oh, I don't know.'

Gracie chimed in. 'Muggles love three things: 'aving their shiny, muggle things; seein' us without them shiny things; and givin' us potato 'cos of all that muggle guilt.'

'You've changed your tune.' Red addressed her. 'Have you forgotten the code? What happened to "God bless the Muggles"? So what, they're our enemy now?'

'Idiot,' said Gracie. 'They ain't the enemy. God bless the Muggles!! They give us wot we need. But don't be thinkin' we give 'em nowt in return. They're very happy with 'ow this all works.'

The young man glanced in the direction of the Arndale and the steps leading up to its entrance, about 100 yards away. There was a beggar there, hunched, shuffling from foot to foot with a plastic cup held out for the benefactions of shoppers passing by. Most came from those who were leaving, weighed down with bags, even if it meant a struggle to dig out money from pocket, purse or wallet.

'You see,' said Bart, standing now and holding forth as if he were lecturing at university, 'You might think of us as "non-contributors", but we're very much part of the economy. We're part of the market rules – if we weren't contributors, this little niche that we support would have ceased to exist long ago.'

'Niche?'

'The charity sector.' The old man smiled. 'Have you ever thought, dear boy, about how the charities are funded?'

'Erm, donations?'

'That is a component, yes. But for homeless charities, it's not the majority. Most of it comes from government grants. Housing foundations are invited to bid for funding; they can apply for capital grants, one-off awards and so on. So now we have a system where charities operate as businesses, competing for grants. They are driven by financial concerns; they hire CEOs, marketing people. Whatever you may think, Red, these charities are not tiny concerns operating out of the goodness of people's hearts. There are 170,000 charities registered in the UK, and the sector is worth £50bn a year.'

Red cast Bart a dubious look after his statistical antics with the police officer.

'Those figures are genuine. It is a massive industry and a highly profitable one at that – in conventional terms. If any business has to pay nothing in tax and gets its products donated for free, it'll do very nicely. And why do they pay no tax? Precisely because of people like you,' he pointed, 'and me. Our lives – our perceived misfortune – form the concept upon which the whole structure persists.'

'But the people who work in these charities, volunteering...'

'Don't get me wrong. Volunteers do want to help. Or at least their guilt wants them to.' He smiled again. 'But so much the better for the charity sector – it has employees working for free.'

'It's too much this, Bart. It's too cynical.'

'Tell that to Socrates.'

'Who?' His head was spinning. He couldn't decide whether what they were telling him was absolute rubbish or the greatest revelation he'd ever heard.

'Do you know that there are housing landlords who operate

as "charities", with fully approved status, mind you, who get a homeless to provide their name, then claim housing benefits using that name, in return for providing said homeless with some basic accommodation at a fraction of the cost?'

'Told yer, didn't I? Never give away yer name!' barked Gracie. 'It's worth more than you are.'

'So you're telling me all this,' answered Red, having heard them out, 'but what do you want me to do about it? What should we do about it?'

'Nuthin',' said Gracie. 'The system works for us too. I don't wanna be "homed".'

'I know! You have said about a *gazillion* times.'

'Nor does B 'ere.'

'Just don't think you are the subject of charity, to be pitied,' said Bartholomew. 'Or, for that matter, a problem to be cured. We are an inherent characteristic of society.'

'Either we've fucked up or been fucked up.'

'Alright, alright... stop ganging up on me. Like being back at school. I'm not an idiot, you know.'

Gracie snorted. 'Five minutes ago, you was all fer givin' yer name to some jobsworth in a uniform.'

The young man was quiet. He still felt embarrassed at how easily his principles had caved when threatened with arrest. Plus, yielding his identity would have made him more vulnerable, not less. If it were not for his companions, he would be kicking round a cell.

It had been a day of learning and humbling, that was for sure. Perhaps there was a vein of truth running through Bart's reasoning; just when Red thought he'd understood the homeless life, a whole new dimension presented itself. Muggles are happy for us to live like this. Charities are dedicated to the bottom line. A name can be worth more than a human being.

Back by the canal, the debate went on long into the evening: Bartholomew expanding on his theories, Red countering the more preposterous parts, Gracie harassing and abusing the pair of them.

After a while, the old man joked: 'There's not a muggle in the land who would expect to hear this conversation going on between three hobos sat round a fire!'

'We're no different to anyone else. Deep down,' said Red. His cheeks shone in the warm light.

'We are!' said Gracie. 'We're better!'

'What I mean is we're not all uneducated, psychotic, and covered in vomit.'

'There's still plenny like that. But yeah,' she said. 'We can string a thought or two together. Hey, B,' she went on, turning to her oldest companion. 'Fancy singin' us a song? I've had enough of us gabbin' for one day. And we need to celebrate pissin' off the Gimps.'

'I didn't know you could sing, Bart,' said Red.

'Many would agree with you–'

'O' course he can sing!' Gracie retorted. 'B is an *ahr*tist.'

The white-haired beggar removed his cap and gave a gracious bow. 'It is a little while since my last performance, but we will see if the old voice holds up. What shall I sing?' He smiled. 'I do requests.'

'Sing *The Manchester Angel*, B. Go on, sing it!'

'*The Manchester Angel*?' said Red. 'Never heard of it.'

'Well, it's about time you did then!'

'Ah, Gracie, you always ask for that one. That and *Dirty Old Town*.' He turned to Red. '*The Manchester Angel* is a folk song handed down for generations round these parts. And it goes something like this–'

Pressing his hands together, the old boy began gently, singing with such sweetness that it took the young man by surprise.

Growing stronger, the sound travelled over the lapping waters and black spaces beneath the bridge.

> I came down to Manchester to find my liberty,
>   And met a pretty girl, full of wild beauty,
> Yes, I met a pretty girl, the prettiest ever I see.
> An Angel of Manchester, she is the girl for me.

Red looked across at Gracie. Her face shimmered with pleasure, lost in the man's performance.

Closing his eyes against the whistle of the wind, folding together his bloated, grimy fingers, listening to those ancient words about eternal things, Red felt a curious sensation coming up from his scuffboot feet, tingling, propagating. He could have been asked a thousand times, but he would never have been able to say what it was or where it came from. Was it the sudden knowledge he had gained? The companionship of these two down-and-outs, these rebels of the world? Maybe it was the adrenaline of almost being arrested, still flowing in the blood. Or was it the unexpected beauty of this voice, this song? The thought of a wild, pretty girl, an Angel of Manchester?

> Then early next morning, at the break of day,
> I went to my Angel's side, my vows to pay,
> I hugged her, I cuddled her, I bade her to lie warm;
> And said, 'I am here to keep you from harm.'

All Red knew was that he could have soared into the air with the euphoria that pitched and danced within him. It was something like love. True, true love. A love of the Street, of this terrible, dirty life. Brutal, inconsequential, pitiable life. This *shelter* from life. But he was convinced, more than ever now, that this *was* life, this was living as he'd never known before.

An open sky was better than an unloving roof. Hunger was better than emptiness, filth better than sterility, violence better than indifference.

Bartholomew had reached the last phrase, and Red felt his eyes madly stinging in the air. His entire being yelled its vagabond joy under the white-starred heavens.

POETRY

It was as winter deepened that Red became ill for the first time. The cold had found his bones and would not let go. Foolish thoughts that he might die entered his head, abetted by strange dreams where he stood, waiting, on the cusp between life and death states. Despite everything he had said to Gracie about continuance, about demise not meaning dissolution, he could not batten down his fear.

There was a day when the shivering in his limbs would not stop, and he could hear the worry in Bartholomew's voice as the old man spoke with him. The young woman was quiet by contrast, and she moved about efficiently, with a tender touch, checking his forehead for fever, propping his head with bags and spare clothes, and covering him with blankets from the local mission. She disappeared for a couple of hours and returned with various medicines, including paracetamol, prepared them for him, ordered him to swallow and sat wordlessly by him until late. What food they had went to him and the old man, and he got a withering look when he protested.

'You should tell more people about it. The code.' The drugs had taken effect and Red had stopped sweating. He felt close to being human again. Being ill had given him plenty of time to think.

'Tell 'em wot?'

'I mean share it.'

'Give over. There's nowt special 'bout it,' she said. 'It's all obvious stuff.'

'If there's nothing special about it, why have you given it such a

fancy title? "The Code". I mean, what are you, God or something?'
Red paused. He was sincere. 'Sometimes it's not about what is
said. It's the fact it's said at all. I don't know. Maybe it would help
other people. When they first come onto the streets. One thing I
do know – when I landed here, I knew nothing.'

'Yer still do. And I shouldn't 've given you them tablets.
They've sent yer daft.'

A week passed before the topic came up again, and in the
meantime, she'd clearly been thinking it over, as she said: 'You
know the code... if I did share it – like you said – well, how d'yer
share somethin' like that?'

He pinched his lower lip, thinking. 'The housing charities
have notice boards, don't they? Or those little wall boxes with
flyers in. Why don't you make some for that?'

'Some wot?'

'Copies. Of the code. So people can read it.'

She considered. 'Guess I could. But I never wrote it out before.'

'I can help. If you'd like.'

Although there was no shortage of paper scraps or used
cardboard to be found blowing about the pavements of
Manchester or in the large rubbish bins which lined its alleys, Red
felt that the code deserved better. For three nights straight, even
in his convalescence, while the chill of the season gripped each
and every evening, the young man walked the streets, hustling
for funds in the dark just as he'd hustled in the day. No freshly
scarred assailant jumped him at any point, but he made sure a
small knife he had bought was stashed in his pocket whenever
he set out, just in case.

The owner of the stationer's shop had regarded him with
distaste and suspicion when he'd presented the fruits of his work
at the counter, along with a basket of purchases, but the coins he
held in his outstretched hand were as good as anyone's, and she
took them, taking care not to touch a beggar boy's palm.

'So that's why you've been out and about till all hours.' Bart nodded approvingly as Red removed the items from his pockets. There were pens, an A5-sized pad of white cards and a box of plastic wallets, also A5 in size.

An unexpected joy shone in Gracie's eyes as she caught sight of them, and she smiled warmly at Red.

'Thank you.'

'Pleasure,' he mumbled.

'You write it,' she said, handing him a pen and one of the cards. 'Yer'll do it better than me.'

The cold made it difficult to write anything at all, but he persevered, transcribing the code word for word as she spoke.

''Ang on,' she said when he was partway through one card. 'It's not quite right. It needs summat at the start. For whoever's readin' it.'

'Whatever are you on about?'

'Shush.'

Bart interrupted: 'Maybe I can help here. I think this calls for some verse, which I used to write myself in the old days.' After some contemplation, he began:

> To you who have no home
> No room to call your own
> To you who walk the streets
> And have no bed in which to sleep
> To you who left the strife
> Of that sorry other life
> To you who have no clue
> On how or what to do
> We offer up this humble code
> For getting by on the beggar's road.

Red was ready to look askance at Gracie, for it seemed to him unnecessarily long, and he didn't know whether it would fit on the card. He also wasn't convinced that the likely readership was into rhyming verse unless it took the form of a rap. But when he turned to look at her, the young woman's eyes gleamed again with excitement, and a grin split across her face. 'It's brilliant, B,' she said. 'I love it!'

Bartholomew tried to look modest.

'We'll write that on one side,' she went on, 'and then the code on the other!'

Clamping the pen once more between numb fingers, Red duly obliged, inscribing the old man's contribution on one side and then, in script which was beginning to slant and flow, Gracie's dictated principles on the other. When he'd finished, he laid down the pen and read them back.

> One: never bum from a bum
> Two: beggars can't be choosers
> Three: God bless the Muggles
> Four: clean kids are mean kids
> Five: there is safety in numbers
> Six: eat or be worm's meat
> Seven: a newspaper is an insulator
> Eight: layers are saviours
> Nine: give use to the useless
> Ten: a shark is a wolf is a shark
> Eleven: trust not the Gimps
> Twelve: shelter from life

'There are some they won't understand,' Red commented. 'Some I barely understand myself.' He laughed. 'Should we change any?'

'No chance! That's the code, 'ow it's always been. If they don't get it, they'll soon learn. Didn't take you long to learn wot a muggle is, did it?'

'How many copies do you want?'

The card slotted neatly into the plastic wallet, and he turned it in his hands, then passed it to Gracie, who also flipped it over a couple of times, admiring, before passing it to Bart, who did the same. Red picked up the pen and the pack of remaining cards, awaiting instructions.

'All of 'em.'

'All of them?' He'd bought a pack of 25 cards.

'Course.'

'Someone's changed their tune.'

'Eh?'

'Before, you weren't sure about doing it at all; now we're writing out 25. Double-sided.'

'If a thing's worth doin', it's worth doin' proper,' she admonished. 'Am I right, B?'

'You're always right, Gracie dear.'

'I'm getting picked on here, I know that.' said Red. 'Look at that handwriting. You not impressed?'

'Wot d'yer want, a chufty badge?'

He smiled and set to writing.

BOBBINS

They went round the charities and soup kitchens, wallets in hand. Each place took a couple for pinning up or as handouts, seemingly unfussed one way or the other, and before long, they'd managed to give quite some coverage to central Manchester's homeless hotspots. A few copies remained. Gracie kept one for herself, and one went in a telephone box. Another three were put on the top decks of buses standing empty in the Gardens before their next loop of the city, on the off chance that they found their way into the hands of itinerants as they travelled in, just as Red had done.

The speed with which the copies left the charitable establishments took all of them by frank surprise; none remained after a week. While Bartholomew was triumphant and Red pronounced himself vindicated, Gracie speculated that they'd been popular for the wallets themselves, as opposed to the contents. Nevertheless, it didn't stop her from wanting to make more. She seemed bitten by this new bug. Some longer hours begging, another pack of cards and wallets, a cramping of ink-stained fingers, and one more tour of the city saw the stock replenished and the experiment extended.

The appetite for their consumption did not diminish, and Red was seriously beginning to wonder what he'd got himself into when one of the charities – who had also noticed the demand – asked Gracie if she might come and talk to people about it at one of their coffee mornings. She had rejected the idea immediately, seemingly petrified. Nothing Red said would change her mind.

'You thought even sharing the code was pointless. And look

what happened!'

'I ain't doing it.'

'It'll help people. To hear you explain things.'

'Not doing it.'

'You need to bring it to life for people. Otherwise, it's merely a piece of paper.'

'Stop peckin'! I. Am. Not. Doing. It. End of!' At which point she stomped off.

In the end, it was Bartholomew who managed to bring her round, exerting, not for the first time, the magical influence which he seemed to hold over her. Red might have guessed that his arm-twisting would begin with a quote, and the old man had lectured:

'"No man is an island, entire of itself. Every man is a piece of the continent, a part of the main. Any man's death diminishes me because I am involved in mankind. And therefore never send to know for whom the bell tolls; it tolls for thee."'

'I ain't a man,' Gracie retorted.

'It's John Donne.'

'It's bobbins, is wot it is.'

But the very next morning, she told Red that she was going to do it. She took full advantage of his mute surprise to warn him not to come and watch. 'On pain of death.'

It was entirely in keeping with the principles of the code that authority be challenged, so he ignored her orders and followed at a suitable distance.

In the modest room reserved for coffee mornings, a crowd of vagrants had gathered. Not one of them was familiar; they were new arrivals on the streets of the metropolis. Young, inexperienced, vulnerable, they were a captive audience for what Gracie was about to say. No one had turned to look as Red entered the room last, taking a seat. Her eyes flashed at the moment of recognition, but he simply nodded and smiled.

She was nervous. Her hands moved constantly. She hopped from one leg to the other. It was another side to Gracie that he hadn't seen: she was normally at ease in her surroundings, confident in its navigation, practised in its challenges. Although it was strange to think that someone could excel at vagrancy, her knack for living on the streets was comparable to a professional skill or an artistic talent; but translating all of that knowledge into a presentation the group could appreciate was something else. Perhaps he should never have encouraged her. What if people switched off? Walked out?

'Hi, everyone. I'm Gracie,' she said. 'I've lived on the streets of Manchester for years now. I... they asked me 'ere to talk about wot I've learned. A few weeks back, I wrote down 12, sort of, rules that I 'ave. That I live by.' Her voice wavered. Her neck had flushed red, and it was approaching her cheeks. The piece of card that she had kept for herself, with its plastic wallet protecting the handwritten contents, was in her hand, and she looked at it, transfixed. Again, her eyes met his, a picture of uncertainty, and he held her stare boldly, willing her to continue.

'No one understands – no one can understand – unless they've stood in these shoes. In your shoes. Only you know why yer life is like it is. And you're the only one who has any answers.'

Red caught himself looking round the circle of people, wondering at the stories that lay behind the faces: the variety of starting points, this shared staging post, their still-to-be-written fates. His own journey came to mind with a renewed clarity, but only as warm, churning chaos, a sequence of events, without any clinching insight as to why its twists and turns had led him to this exact spot: sitting, watching this woman, whom he'd met at random after an impulse to abandon his surroundings. He didn't know whether that sense of helpless disarray was peculiar to the homeless existence or could be extended to the rest of humanity.

'One,' Gracie was saying. 'Never bum from a bum.'

Suddenly it was as though the difficult terrain had levelled out, and her footing gained smooth and solid ground. The breathless quality of her delivery dissipated; her head came up; she took her time to speak. She was into her flow, and the audience listened with rapt attention.

'We're all bums, 'bonds, beggars, and it's nuthin' to be ashamed of. It's who we are. But we mustn't ever bum from one another. Who begs from a beggar? That's like trying to take medicine from a sick person. No, no, we bum from the muggle!'

A hand came up. 'What's a muggle?'

'Well–'

It was the last of the principles that generated the most interest. They went up to her afterwards, keen to hear more about how she had made this way of life a sustainable thing and how they could do likewise. He understood it. How it resonated with the newly homeless. Refuge from the past – from the misery they had come from, in each and every story – was exactly what they craved.

Red wasn't sure that the charities felt the same way. He'd watched the staff throughout the speech Gracie had given, and they'd looked uncomfortable at that piece, as well as the preceding rule about not trusting the police.

'Perhaps you should get rid of rules 11 and 12 from the code,' he said a couple of days later.

'Why?'

'The charities won't want to be seen supporting those ideas: "Cops are untrustworthy, oh and stay on the Street!" They'll be wanting to encourage the opposite.'

She considered for a moment. 'They are the truth. I ain't changing them for nobody. I'm not gunna lie to people. Plus, *they* invited *me*! They knew wot were in the code. It's all or nuthin'.'

Whether it was because they didn't care as much as he thought or because there was a demand that they couldn't ignore, the charity asked Gracie to speak again. As the weeks passed, he could feel a momentum growing, that something of importance was being developed; whether it would become more than the cards that he continued to write out and the periodic sessions that she continued to hold, he didn't know. He could see she was happy though, and Bartholomew too, and that was all that mattered.

'They've asked me to speak at the Christmas party at Hope Mission,' she said one day.

'Really?' said Red. 'That's great news. Bart can play Father Christmas.'

BARD

Christmas day was the one day of the year when, as a homeless, you could be sure of a full stomach. As in muggle life, effort was poured into making a dinner to remember. Every charity and shelter which could provide cooked food did so, hour after hour, until the demand had gone. It was the day of festive cheer when all grievances were supposedly put out of reach and inequalities banished. The 'bonds and bums filed into canteen halls to sit shoulder to shoulder. Festive cheer still had its limits: there was no alcohol allowed or served, and anyone showing signs of inebriation was sent packing.

Gracie was sat to Red's left, talking loudly to the woman beside her. Bartholomew was opposite, his face red and glistening from the heat of room and the pleasure bubbling inside him. There was only one thing on Red's mind: the food that lay before him. As he glanced up, registering the other homeless that were filling benches the length of the room, he picked out those individuals poised like himself over their plate, consciously drowning out the hum of voices around them, engaged in quasi-spiritual anticipation of the communion to come.

At some point in every day, hunger held an impossible grip over you. The regularity of its control waned as your appetite declined beyond normal human needs, but when it struck, it was desperate, an obsession, heightened by the perpetual cold, and commingled with the feelings of hopelessness which were never far away. Perhaps because they had been on the Street for longer, Gracie and Bart did not seem to suffer as much as he did. Or maybe they just hid it better.

The saliva leapt into his mouth, and he found his hands shaking as he gripped the cutlery. But he would not be rushed. Each slice of the knife, each loading of the fork, would be undertaken with ecstatic precision. He could visualise the soft, gravied morsels entering his mouth and the precious flavours clinging to his palate; he could foretaste that consecrated warmth, the gloried textures, the terrible bliss of a stomach which was full, memorably full.

There were three lustrous tranches of turkey layered, one on top of another. Carefully he separated them, devouring the smallest first, nicking and cutting with concentration lest a shred of meat be missed. The pigs-in-blankets needed cooking longer, as the fatty bacon rind lay thick and white around the sausage, but there was no room for squeamishness; he ate it all, relishing the grease on his lips and teeth. The parsnips, potatoes and sprouts were less interesting on the way down but weighed beautifully in his stomach. The cranberry sauce was sugar-sweet, the Yorkshire puddings doughy. Christmas pudding and custard were despatched with the same diligence and reverence, and before Red knew what was happening, tears sprang to his eyes, and he had to lower his head to brush them away with a napkin.

One final act before it all became memory: a quarter of the Christmas pudding, soaked in custard to keep it moist, went into his napkin, and from there, into the pocket of his coat. Then he sat back, stretching his legs under the table. It was as though someone had pulled a cord on all the tension in his body, on those perpetually hunched shoulders, on that wary, circumspect countenance, and he couldn't stop his muscles from relenting, slumping, giving up the ghost. Sleep could have overtaken him, sleep from magnificent, paralysing contentment... He burped and was too tired to laugh.

'Well that were pretty effin' good,' said Gracie, laying down her spoon.

Bartholomew agreed. 'One of the finest that I've had since, well, last year.' He grinned, eyes shining.

The charity had arranged for Gracie to hold a session in one of the rooms once lunch had concluded, and she headed over there while Red and Bart remained in their seats talking.

'She's a natural,' Red said. 'I hadn't realised it before.'

'It's good for her.' He rubbed at his beard. '"The busy bee has no time for sorrow."'

'Shakespeare?'

'Another William.'

'Why do you like your quotes so much, Bart?'

'Quotations. Oh, I don't know, my dear chap. What's not to like? Great minds wrapped up in a line.'

'And Shakespeare?'

'The Bard. Ah. That dates back to my teenage years. I told you I was a reader, I think. A lonely fellow. I came across him in lessons at school and then devoured the rest myself. It wasn't reading, you see, not that. It was spiritual. Everything was so perfectly written – when I say perfect, I mean like little drops of beauty and revelation about who I was, all rolled into one. Do you follow?'

'I think so.'

'Strange to love the thoughts of a fellow from 500 years ago. But there we are. Nothing can be done about it.'

'It's unusual, I'll give you that. A Shakespeare-loving tramp.' He gave a short laugh. 'If you know what I mean.'

'I do. But I'm homeless, not illiterate. Being homeless has not reduced me. Quite the reverse. You're still the same person, aren't you? As when you left home.'

'I guess,' the young man said, though he wasn't entirely sure.

'The essence remains. It's what our homed friends do not understand. "If you prick me, do I not bleed?"' He laughed. 'I have one for every occasion.' He paused, his attention reverting to Gracie, who was still holding court. 'You've been good for her, you know. She is better now. Better than she used to be. You don't realise it because you never knew her before you came, but you coming along the way you have has been a new beginning for her.'

'I've done nothing,' said the youngster. Truly he believed that. 'You're the ones who took me in when I was in need.'

There was a long silence. Then Red said: 'Does she like me?'

'Of course she likes you.'

'No, I mean "like" like.'

'Oh. I don't know. With Gracie, I think it's more faith in humanity,' he said. 'Romance... I don't know. Well, it's sort of... secondary. Something buried rather deep. For her. When you've been through what she has. But she does like you; she honestly does.'

'I don't know if I meant romance.' Red found it difficult to say the word; he felt a prickle of embarrassment.

'Do you know my favourite quote?' asked Bart.

'Go on.'

'It's Blaise Pascal. "The heart has its reasons, of which reason knows nothing".'

The old man had grown pensive; their conversation, man and boy, had him thinking about other conversations he could have been having. Conversations between a father and son. 'I wonder,' he said slowly, 'what he's doing today.'

'Don't get yourself down, B.'

'Indeed, my friend.' He pulled at his jumper, and some crumbs of Yorkshire pudding fell to the ground. 'My son will be all grown up. I imagine how he might be.' He gave a disappointed smile. 'The fate of an absentee father.'

'Well, your parents can be present and still be absent.' The young man paused. 'You never know. Maybe, at this very moment, he's thinking about his dad.'

'Thank you, dear chap.' The tramp's eyes twinkled as though recalling some special memory. 'I feel it, sometimes.' With a slow nod he raised his weathered hand and tapped his chest. 'Across the distance.' He took himself outside for a smoke; the emotions were getting too much for him.

The emotion had gotten to Red too. For the second time in an afternoon, his eyes were wet. He laid his hands on the table, their plain, dirty contours rasping the wood. There was everything to remember in those few seated seconds, everything to treasure, and he wished he could capture it, seal it up, impervious to all harm past and present.

But it all vanished the day that Bartholomew died.

THUMB

The loss of her ectopic had not been Shane's first taste of grief. That had come a decade earlier with the death of her father. From the age of five, she had understood that this would happen, that her parents would grow old and die, but it was a concept in the ether, and no amount of rehearsal, in moments of quiet reflection, had prepared her for the day.

She had been at his bedside when he passed. Death approached doggedly for hours before it landed; when it came, the pale, bleak transformation of her father could not be reconciled with the living man she'd known. How could such a vital personality just disappear?

In the waxen face and hardened limbs, she found no hint of continuity. Only rupture. Severance. At first, she had been unable to grasp it; such terminality was as alien and as opaque to reason as the infinity of numbers. Life stood in contrast – as a warm, indefinite thresh, where human experience never stopped, and all but the worst situation might promise hope.

So why do you care about the dead, she asked herself. They travel into the quietus. They cannot be helped at all. But knowing is seldom acting; reason and feeling rarely align; she couldn't stand by and do nothing. And that was the heart of her dilemma: a living woman applying the rules of life to the remains of the dead.

Without telling a soul of her intentions, she went to the NatWest branch in Chinatown. Her idea was the smallest act of rebellion ever conceived, but she was convinced that it was the right thing to do. She had not failed Red so far, and she would not fail him here either.

The clerk filed her nails while she processed the withdrawal of £2000. Shane had never seen so much cash in a single, rubber-banded wad before, and she couldn't help feeling like a drug mule as she slipped it into her handbag and left the premises.

The funds had not come from hers and Ryan's joint account; they were from the savings account she'd opened up before they had met. Building any savings had taken Shane a long time; she had often imagined how they might be spent in the way that stored money gets put to a hundred fantasies of use. The one thing she had not earmarked it for was a funeral.

Don't get mugged, she told herself as she returned to the offices in St Peter's Square.

The withdrawal sat under her desk for the rest of the afternoon, like some dirty secret harbouring beside her feet. She grew tense when Martin approached to talk about the assignment of two new cases. The rebellion might be small, but she could not deny the bubble of anticipation when she thought of everything it represented.

The council used an undertaker on Barlow Moor Road, not far from Southern Cemetery; the sign, J Sampson & Sons, was written in calligraphic font, and the windows had solemn, half-closed blinds. She remembered that there'd been some localised uproar in the Metro, or maybe the Gazette, a few years back when the contract first got awarded because Mr J Sampson was the brother-in-law of one of the councillors. It had not stopped matters going ahead of course, once the noise had died down, and now there was a thriving chain of establishments.

'I work for the council,' Shane said. 'The Deceased Affairs Office. I'm here about a public health burial.'

'I see. How can I help?' The woman behind the desk had spoken each word in deft, dampened tones, as though she didn't want to wake the dead ranged in the back. Her curly dark hair sprung gently as she lowered her glasses from the top of her head onto the tip of her nose and watched the DAO through them.

The scheduling of a 'pauper's funeral' was outside of a DAO's control. Once the council had provided the rudimentary details and released the body, the undertaker took over all arrangements. A date would have been fixed with the cemetery and a basic coffin ordered up. That was as far as it went: there would be no gravestone and no service.

Shane took a slip of paper from her trouser pocket. It was the case reference number. She also drew the money from her handbag.

'We had an envelope delivered to the council offices. An anonymous benefactor enclosed money and instructions. They have requested an engraved headstone and an upgraded casket.'

'The burial is scheduled for this Thursday,' the woman said. 'I'm afraid we will not be able to meet those timeframes.'

Shane delicately explored options for expediting the order. In the end, there'd been a premium to pay, but she had succeeded. Cash was still very much the language of the living, even in the affairs of the dead.

Only then did she tell someone the truth: the sexton. He alone, as a survivor of the Street, could understand why she was doing what she was. He had listened, nodded, arranged for a conversation with the priest.

At the appointed time, the man of God was completing a funeral, so Shane waited on the cemetery grounds. The day was sharp and cold. The sky was white without any of the brightness, and the wind was plaintive through the treetops. From the open church doors, a procession emerged; she heard the threads of incantation carried in the air, those age-old rhythms of the service for the dead. The coffin was borne on four staunch shoulders, and the mourners followed slowly in aching disorder. Dressed all in black, some wore stoic faces, while others crumpled at the mouth or let their eyes run amid the rending sounds. Poor people, Shane thought, though it was how things should be. It should matter when someone leaves the Earth. The closer they had been to the departed, the more stunned and stricken they would be; the longer it would take for their disbelief to die and for acceptance to begin. For some, the grief was never fully spent, though the years continued to march on.

The priest and the DAO talked in the sexton's room, among the shelving and the records.

'A young man is being buried. Red Milliner.' She held out the money. 'This is for the service.' Her bag was considerably lighter now. There would not be much left after this. The expenses had soon mounted: the coffin, its exterior and interior furnishings; the gravestone and its lettering; the flowers and the wreaths; a payment to secure the burial plot.

The clutch of notes was clumsy in her hands. He, too, was the recipient of the fiction about a mysterious benefactor. For a split second, she apprehended the madness of what she was doing. It wasn't exactly the crime of the century; in fact, it wasn't a crime at all, but it was a misrepresentation of the truth. Perhaps it was a white lie?

She could feel him studying her. As a child, Shane had gone to a Roman Catholic school, and her mother had taken her to church every Sunday. But when she'd hit her teenage years, and especially when she'd moved away from home, she'd found herself attending less and less amid a blossoming of doubt, and she sensed the priest divining this: there were words waiting in his eyes, words of keen reproach, or commiserating sorrow, for a woman who'd lost her way.

Lost her way. He had no idea.

It was no longer a matter of young agnosticism or seesawing faith, of questions about origins and afterlives. It was no longer a question of churchgoer or pagan.

How would he react if he heard about her baby? If she showed her anger? What were his thoughts on failed implantation? If there was Design going on there, then it had to be the cruellest variety, for it was a life wickedly ended before it began.

His fingers fastened around the little knot of money, the eyes turning away, keeping their counsel, and matters were concluded.

The day of Red's funeral arrived. The rain had paused for breath. Southern Cemetery twittered and shone as Shane trod the short stone path to the church doors. The grass that peeled away on both sides was well-tended. It undulated gently before meeting the headstones that reached up from the earth.

The cemetery had been established in the middle of the 19th century, part of that great Victorian wave of sanitising the graveyard spaces. Proper civil planning had meant landscaped terminals for the departed to rest and for the grieving to pay their respects. In those days, it had absorbed the great and good of Manchester's community, great in coin and good of credit. Then purchases of land had enabled it to grow. Now there were two separate chapels for holding services, and it was no longer just cotton merchants who reposed in its grounds. There was even room for the Nameless to be buried, and it made for quite a sea of tombstones for the surveying eye.

The DAO had played a role in the interment of many nameless, but this was the first where she had organised every aspect of the service. It was the first that she had ever paid for.

Red was no longer nameless, of course, but there was almost nothing she could tell the priest about the young man's life: some basic facts about his birth and death, his schooling, the place he'd grown up, that he'd run away from home; that he'd met Gracie. The single school photo of him was projected onto a screen behind the altar.

It was all so insubstantial that Shane began to wonder whether she had done the right thing in trying to do this her way. Could she bring dignity to Red's memory when there was so little to remember him by? There was a wealth to his story, hinted at in the possessions that he'd left behind, which she'd been unable to bring to life.

His parents were absent. In the end, his dental records supplied the means of identification as they had refused to view his body. It couldn't be right that in the whole church, not one soul had known the figure whose life was being commemorated, yet there was only the priest, the pallbearers, the sexton, a handful of active members of the parish and Shane herself.

A year or so before, Gracie's farewell had been held on the same grounds, and she wondered whether it had drawn a similar crowd or if it was as nebulous a life account. The sister of a murdered infant, the author of the Beggar's Code, Gracie had borne tragedy and hardship that no service could convey, but on the day she'd been laid to rest, at least one person present had known her. Red would have entered the church doors, sat in one of the pews, as groomed and smart as circumstances would allow, all to mark the life of someone who had mattered. He had paid for the privilege.

But then the young man had mattered to Shane, whether she'd known him alive or not. Perhaps this was some sort of answer, then: remembrance might be more than the look-back at a life. It was a signal of its importance.

Why had he been important?

The Deceased Affairs officer looked up at the church ceiling, its high rafters and lonely, suspended lights, and she could find only one answer, that she'd been *able* to do this thing for him. She had become tired of the things she could *not* do. This was different; it was fitting, it was right. With what he'd sacrificed for Gracie, someone had to give him the self-same due, even if it was a person he'd never met.

The sexton glanced at her and gave a short nod. The hymns began; the priest spoke. There were readings about death not being the end, about souls being welcomed into eternal bliss and about the special place that He reserves for all.

The feet of the pallbearers crunched the gravelled road as they headed to the assigned plot, just as they had the day she'd waited for the priest, except this time, she was part of the procession. Shane had ordered a casket of good quality oak, with brass handles and a velvet lining; there were wreaths for the coffin to match the bouquets which had lined the church. A hole in the ground loomed ahead of them suddenly, the dark mouth ready to receive. Then Red's coffin was lowered on the ropes, and the earth was put in the hole. The priest said his final words.

Freshly cut with the young man's name, the grave looked bright and clean under the cemetery sky. Next to it was Gracie's simple marker. Red was being buried in the plot next to hers: he was not going to ground with a cursory ceremony, he was not going unlabelled, and he would not be unaccompanied.

The sun was bolder now, illuminating, searching out the shadows between the two vagabonds lying side by side.

Now things were complete. Shane rested a gentle hand on her stomach, and a feeling of peace rose within her.

ROSE

Of the tragedy to come, Red saw no sign on the horizon. The first portents came one evening when he and Gracie returned from begging for handouts. Bartholomew was nowhere to be found.

His possessions were still in their usual place under the canal bridge, and there were clues he'd been interrupted in the midst of his activities: the tattered fishing chair was open, a depression in the seat from where he'd been sitting close to the water, and beside it, a half-smoked cigarette floated in the puddle where it had fallen.

Instinctively Red's eyes scanned the surface in case the old man had fallen in, but amid the bobbing cans, plastic bags and branches, he caught no glimpse of a human shape, of fabric or flesh.

After a minute or so of searching, they found him face down and motionless on an embankment less than 50 yards away in the shadow of a construction site for apartment blocks. They ran to him. At first, it seemed like a heart attack or stroke, but his eyes were open, and he was still breathing; he simply didn't respond, no matter how much they shook him and called his name. Red had never seen anything like it, but Gracie knew exactly what it was.

'Spice.'

He saw instantly that she was right. Bart had the same blanched, cadaverous face and calcified limbs of all those wretches they had observed in the back alleys and disused vistas of the city. It was the zombification that the old man himself had often warned them about.

Red scooped Bartholomew under his arms, and Gracie grabbed his ankles; they lugged him down the embankment. With a little effort, they had him in the recovery position, hidden away beneath the bridge, on a rolled-out sleeping bag. She stooped momentarily, rummaging through his pockets. Then they took themselves to the railing at the edge of the canal to talk. His curiosity was piqued as she fished the cigarette from the puddle on her way.

'He smoked it.' She unrolled the cigarette paper, and the young man noticed flecks of green among the brown tobacco. He realised now that she'd been hunting for the tobacco pouch while checking his pockets; she produced it now.

The pouch was mostly empty, but in the curled, wiry remnants, they saw the same green flecks of Spice resting with a harmless glint among the brown.

'But he always told us not to get involved with drugs.'

She was silent momentarily, then shook her head. 'I don't think 'e knew 'e were smoking it. It were put in here, and then he mustn't have seen it when he rolled 'is cigarette.'

'So someone spiked the pouch. That's what you're saying.' The shock spread across Red's face. 'I bet it was Darren, wasn't it?' Gracie wouldn't look at him. 'Don't you see? It must be him. Bart said he'd told him to sling his hook.'

''E wouldn't 'ave done that.'

'But who else–'

'No!' The young woman erupted. The word echoed across the waters like a slap. 'No. It wasn't him.'

'How can you be sure?'

'I just know. I was mute for a year. Darren brought me back from that. You don't understand. What I owe 'im. Who 'e is. It wasn't him!'

'So who the fuck was it then?'

'It were the Street,' she said, her eyes murky and clouded as they finally met his.

'The Street is not a person.'

'These things happen on the Street. Dealers try to get you

hooked. Yer can never let yer guard down. It 'appens on the Street.'

'"These things happen"... Can you hear yourself? You make it sound like some little accident.'

'Don't fucking lecture me. Bart is my friend. Not yours.'

'He's mine too.'

'Yer know nuthin' about the Street – still, after all this time. Yer knew nuthin' when I saved yer. And yer know nuthin' now.'

While Bartholomew emerged from his coma within a few hours, he experienced a withdrawal which began shortly afterwards and lasted for days. He writhed in his bag, marinating in sweat, his face bloodless and limbs jittering. For the second time in a month, Gracie nursed without fuss or misgiving while Red took to the streets for food and supplies. He begged; he got manual labour unloading trucks; he found a discarded blanket which Gracie propped under the patient's head.

Finally, the visible grip of addiction passed, and their lives went back to the way they'd been before. Bart made no reference to what had happened, and Red couldn't lower the man's dignity further by raising the subject. He and Gracie must have talked about it together, he supposed, but man and boy let the matter lay unspoken between them, as a father and son might, knowing an adventure with words could be more dreadful than the event itself.

A rapidly spreading discourse about the Beggar's Code, mostly among the charity staff and in their community publications, reached the ears of the council, and they clamped down on it, demanding the more controversial content be removed. 'Censorship,' Gracie called it. Bart told her that it was a matter of perceived control: she could cede some ground and still achieve her aims. But she point-blank refused. Copies of the code circulated in a faintly underground fashion. Red wrote out no more because the council had ordered charities not to stock it. A small crowd would congregate impromptu sometimes, there on the towpath, to hear her talk about the code and more besides. Gracie worked hard to project her voice in the open spaces while the assembled stood silently and respectfully to listen.

One day he saw Darren standing at the back of a small group. The villain was wearing a cap, which was the first time Red had seen him with one, but it was him alright. No indication that Gracie saw him. Arriving after she'd begun and leaving before she'd finished, he kept his head low and neck forward, straining to hear. In response to the conduct of the authorities, Gracie's talks had started to become more militant, something that Bart, in particular, warned her against, noting that the power was with those in power and that she, maybe all three of them, would find themselves bothered by the police at some point if she continued. No such discouragement from the crowd, and it was strange to see this short, young woman hold sway with the motley crew before her, punctuating some of her more pointed commentary with a cheer or a smattering of applause. Darren clapped too, and Red caught a glimpse of the lion tattoo as the left sleeve of his jacket rode up before he tugged it down again.

'I saw him,' Red told Bart one evening when Gracie had fallen asleep before them. 'I saw Darren. Two days ago.'

Moving along the deserted towpath, out from under the shadowy bridge and into the stark lamplight, they were out of earshot of the sleeping figure.

'I thought his departure was too good to be true.'

'Same.'

Gracie's furious testimony had not changed Red's mind. He still believed that it was Darren who had spiked Bart's tobacco. If the old man thought likewise, then here was the obvious opening for him to say so. But instead, there was a long silence.

Finally, Bart asked, 'Dear boy. Have you ever been addicted to something?'

'No,' he said, taken aback. 'I don't think so.'

'Then you haven't. You would know.'

'My mother,' Red interrupted. 'She...' He swallowed. 'She is addicted.'

'To what?'

He gave a miserable laugh. 'To her dreams, I suppose.'

'Dreams?'

'Of who she is. Of what she can be, I think. There was always some scheme, you see – to be something. To earn her fortune. Straightforward gambling some of it. Respectable gambling the rest. There was always a pot of gold with her name on it.'

'What about your father?'

'His addiction is my mother. It's bad for both of them.' The insight surprised Red himself: only now could he step back and view his parents with a distanced gaze. So much of what he'd blamed himself for was not his fault. Was not about him at all. In a sense, it was a further hammering of his self-esteem to realise just how peripheral he had been to his parents, that he had not even been the cause of their troubles; in another sense, it was liberating. He had stopped caring. And the secret to freedom, to life itself, was not to care about anything, about anyone. Lost in thought, the young man redoubled his vow to stand alone from the rest of humankind: to never be the victim of love, never be shackled to a marriage and never put a child through what he'd been through.

'There's something missing in your mother,' Bart said. 'Some great unhappiness in her. Addiction has this knack of finding the holes in people.'

'Hm,' answered Red, looking out over the water. 'I do feel sorry for her. She's in a prison.'

'I've made a decision, dear boy. You told me I should seek out my son. I thought about it. You are right, of course. I will find a way. I will do it.'

The practical thoughts of how to raise the money for travel to China and of how to find the boy when he got there seemed to rise in the air between them, as real as any object, before the man said, 'It needs some planning. It's not impossible.'

'No. Not at all. I'll help in any way I can,' Red said.

'It was different before. There was just me and Gracie. But you're here now. You will look after her, won't you?' Worry had returned to the weather-worn face. The crease lines on his forehead overlapped and knotted.

'She doesn't need looking after.'

'Promise!' he urged.

'You haven't gone anywhere yet.'

Don't tie yourself to anyone, the voice came back, just as urgent. It is pain, it is suffering. Don't! It is a prison.

'Yes,' Red said after a long pause. 'Yes, I promise.'

BURIED

The sexton phoned Shane that afternoon.

'Someone called me. They were asking about the funeral. Red's funeral.'

'In what way?'

'About who paid for it.'

'What did you say?'

'An anonymous benefactor. Was that okay?'

'Yes,' she said, though, in truth, she didn't know.

'Sorry. If it gets you into trouble.'

'No, no, it's okay. Was it a man or a woman?'

'A woman.'

'Okay. Thanks.'

He paused. 'You never explained,' he said, 'why you paid for Red's funeral yourself.'

'I don't know. But then, why do we do anything for our dead?' He waited, and she said, 'I don't know if what I did mattered.'

'Hm.' The phone went quiet, then: 'I think it mattered. Matters.'

Martin called her into his office. The truth was out. It might have been the woman at the undertaker's who had flagged her odd behaviour; most likely, it was Bettina Milliner, having learned somehow of her son's upgraded burial. Regardless, it felt inevitable in retrospect, and while the showdown hadn't come before the young man was laid to rest with a full service and headstone, it came hotfoot after.

'How dare you?' His eyes crackled with an anger she'd never seen before. 'Is it true? What I've been told.'

'Who told you?'

'Did you pay for his funeral? The dead homeless?'

Shane felt her own fury building. Red had been a lot more than a 'dead homeless'. 'Yes. I did.' She wasn't about to lie.

'How much?'

'Two grand. And it was worth every – fucking – penny.'

There was silence.

Now that word had been used, he wasn't going to be outdone. 'Who the *fuck* do you think you are?'

She folded her arms and looked away.

He stood up and paced behind his desk. 'You know the pressure I'm under. We're under. In this department. I have Alan in my ear about it 24 hours a day.'

'Not my problem.'

'It's *all* our problem.'

'I saved you money.'

'I told you that the case was over. But you wouldn't listen. You had to prove a point.'

'I was an anonymous benefactor. Remember Gracie's case. You said they do come forward. What's the difference? It happened to be me.'

'You went behind my back–'

'No.'

'You went behind my back. A public health burial wasn't "good enough". You didn't save any money. You embarrassed the council. You embarrassed me!' He pointed a finger. 'You were scoring points. Admit it. You wanted this job. When I got it, you resented it.'

'No!' She was indignant. 'I did what I did because it was the right thing to do. If you can't see that, that's not my fault!'

'It is *not* your job to decide that. You're not some kind of social crusader.'

'So it's wrong to try to make things better?'

'He had a funeral arranged and paid for. By the state.'

'What, a basic box, no headstone, no service to celebrate his life? Some shitty hole in the ground?'

Martin was unmoved.

'So when you die,' Shane stood up now, challenging. She didn't care what they saw or heard outside the glass panel. 'You don't want any of those things? People there, a proper send-off? Some dignity?'

'This has nothing to do with me.'

'He was a human being. Like you.'

'How do you think the press would carry on if they knew about this? Government cuts. Council workers paying for funerals out of their own pocket. Imagine the headlines.'

'Why won't you answer my question?'

The man whom she had always considered a friend shrugged. 'When I die, I don't care what they do with what's left. It really doesn't matter. I won't know a thing about it. We don't do this job for the dead. We sort things out for the sake of the living.' She didn't recognise this side of him. This coldness. 'But what I believe doesn't matter. It is council policy.'

'You were a journalist. You fought for social justice. You cared about Gracie. What has happened to you?'

The man slammed his hand on the desk. 'Don't lecture me! You've been years in this department and never once did this before. All those people who we – who you – never identified. They all went in a hole in the ground. A PBH was bloody well good enough then. What you've done, it's hypocritical.' He was back in control of himself. 'I have never changed my view. We do enough. More than enough. We should focus our resources on the living, not the dead. Which is exactly what departmental policy instructs me to do.'

'It wasn't purely about Red,' Shane said. There was defiance in her voice. 'I couldn't do another one. Another burial like that.' She was struggling to find her words. It was like a physical grip on her neck, her chest. 'I can't do another one.'

He glanced at her. 'What do you mean?'

'You haven't communicated the redundancies yet, have you? I want to be one of them.'

MANDARIN

A week after Bart's episode, just after dusk, Red came across a hastily scribbled note from Gracie. It had been weighted down with a tin can.

'Don't know where B is,' it said. 'Gone to find him.'

Although the derelict building in Chinatown wasn't the last place he would have looked, it wasn't the first that came to mind either, and it was late in the night, or maybe early in the morning, when Red finally tried there. Twice he had gone back to the canal, and they'd still not returned. Something must be very wrong, and the biting worry drove him on. He'd been to every charity and dosshouse that he knew, every stopping-point they'd used along the canal, the disused car parks, the 'empties' around the city. But there was no sign of them. No sign, even, that he was following in the footsteps of Bartholomew or Gracie or both. It was easy to forget how huge Manchester was and the endless possibilities to remain out of sight.

One of the cardinal rules of the Beggar's Code was that there was safety in numbers. As he stood at the entrance to the cavernous, unlit building beneath a peeling oriental sign, he felt the mounting unease of being alone and vulnerable to attack. Could the man who had delighted in disfiguring the Homeless make a vengeful return?

He had the knife with him in his trouser pocket, ready to be grasped. He thought of Gracie on her own and the courage she would have needed to initiate her search for the old man. It seemed to help gather him.

The main doors had been boarded up since he was last here, but more than one of the windows was broken on the ground floor, and their glass pushed out. They were not high, and he pulled himself through with relative ease. A twist of fabric gyrated in the air where it had snagged on a nail in the windowsill; it was dark green and textured like the trousers Bartholomew wore. Red's heart leapt.

There was no artificial light in the building, and the young man had no means of bringing it. There was only the glow and reflection of the streetlamps, the haze of distant tenements and the moon above. It took time for his eyes to adjust and for him to orient himself.

Warily he crossed the floor of the decaying room. Pigeons had been using it as a nesting place and toilet; there were rodents too, and he caught sight of one scurrying across a patch of moonlight. He had thought to call out for Bart and Gracie, but fear held him back. There might be other occupants in the empty, and who knew how they would react. His feet creaked occasionally on the boards. No figure came rushing out from behind the crimson, shredded wall hangings. A wide set of stairs led to an upper floor, and this still had its carpet, deep and rotting, royally red in places. On the wall, stretching the length of the staircase, was the giant mural that he remembered: a mountain scene with a temple sheltering in the lee of an overhanging ledge and gnarled trees clinging to the precipitous rocks. The mandarin script still ran down one side, undiminished, though he could no longer remember what Bart's translation had been.

He reached the top of the stairs. It opened into a second large dining room.

Bartholomew and Gracie were there, alone, in one corner. He could see within a couple of paces that the old man had passed away. He was lying on his side, and his eyes were open. She was still alive, lying on her back, frozen, except for one foot that tremored. There was an empty plastic packet beside the outstretched fingers of her right hand. The writing on it said 'Incense', but he knew that it had held Spice.

Red wept, his grief coming in uncontrollable sobs echoing around the empty structure. With a gentle touch, he closed Bartholomew's eyes. For the second time in his life, he stood over the body of a tramp, but this time it held no morbid fascination; there was only horror and devastation. Nothing could be done.

The need to save Gracie ignited in him like a spark, and he tried to get her to her feet. Trust not the Gimps. If either of them were found near Bartholomew's body, they would be arrested on suspicion of having supplied the drug that had killed him. Leaving his body to be discovered, perhaps some time from now, when the process of decay had set in, and the rodents had begun their work, was unbearable to think of, but they could not stay.

Getting medical help for Gracie was impossible for the same reason, but he hoped the effects would wear off in time. She did not respond to her name. It was terrible to see her in such a state, unable to speak, her eyes rolling back in her head. Draping one of her arms over his neck, he managed to get her up and drag her towards the stairs. The act of motion seemed to stir an automated reaction in her feet, and they straightened, anchoring to the floor like a sleepwalker's. At one point, he felt her fingers move, tightening around his shoulder; but her head lolled, its matted mass of red hair undimmed in the gloom of the building. They fell twice on the stairs. It took a superhuman effort to get her moving again. He looked out of the broken window to check that the alley was deserted before heaving her through and onto the ground beneath.

For a moment, he touched the windowsill. His thumb and forefinger brushed the scrap of fabric that twisted still in the wind. With a terrible sense of finality, he thought of how Bartholomew would never see his son. He also thought of the promise he'd made to the man. 'Goodbye, old friend,' he said. Then he lifted Gracie again, hooking her under one arm, and struggled away down the alley.

'I didn't want 'im goin' through it alone,' she said. Gracie retched. It took two hours before she regained the ability to speak. Dawn had broken. She could move on her own but was dreadfully weak. Her stomach had nothing left to vomit except bile, and she doubled up in pain.

Bartholomew had been dead when she found him. Taking his lighter, she had lit what was left of his cigarette with the Spice rolled in it and smoked it down. Then she'd lain beside him.

'You could have died.'

'I couldn't let 'im go on his own.' She shook her head.

'He was gone,' said Red with bitterness.

'I owed 'im.'

'I don't understand,' he said. 'Why did he take it?' Then: 'He was an addict, wasn't he? I mean. Not just the Spice.'

'When I first met B, he was goin' cold turkey; it was so hard for 'im. He was always hooked on somethin'. That's really why he left China. The thing about his wife findin' someone else weren't a lie, but he was using, it got out o' control. He was gettin' it in the nightclubs. He'd heard the local gimps knew about it, and they don't take that shit lightly over there. 'E went to the airport that fucking day; got the hell out. Didn't want trouble for his son neither. So 'e came here, 'e got clean, and it was his new start. He did want to go back. But then...'

'How could he lie to me?' Red demanded. 'All that time. How could you not tell me?'

''Cos he never wanted yer to know. He didn't want you goin' the same way. And 'e was a proud man. Didn't want you thinking he was some junkie. So he hid it. Made me swear I wouldn't tell yer.' She looked at him with tears in her eyes.

'You said it was the Street that got him onto Spice.'

'So it were.'

'We could have helped him.'

She shook her head.

'All those things he said about freedom,' he went on. 'The quotes. Pretending he was happy.'

'He was better for a bit. We all have secrets, Red. 'E tried his best.'

Try as he might, the young man couldn't reconcile the image of the wise, intelligent man he had known with that concealed history, but then, that knowledge underlined the struggle it must have been.

'I just feel sorry,' said Red.

'What for?'

'What he went through. That he's gone.'

They had reached the back of Piccadilly Train Station. It was bitingly cold, the winds buffeting them from across the open car park. 'The Gimps will find 'im,' she said. 'We need to quit the city. For some time.'

'Where will we go?'

'I don't know.'

Gracie pawed at a strand of hair plastered to her forehead. She looked up. Above them, the ever-present seagulls wheeled and sounded their sad calls.

DENNIS

Shane left the council offices. The idea of sitting at her desk for the rest of the afternoon made her sick to the stomach; she felt rage and loathing, a fulminating conviction about everything she'd done, a disgust that could last and last. She had to be alone. Before she'd even burst out of the front doors, her feet were on their way to Piccadilly Gardens.

The lunch hour had finished, and the Gardens were not exactly busy, though they were never quiet either. Temporary fencing had been put up around the grassy areas, and workmen were chatting as they replaced the worn turf. A one-legged pigeon bobbed towards her, chasing down a sandwich crust; then the swish of a cleaner's broom clacking against a bin had the whole host of birds rocketing into the sky, girding the concrete world before falling to earth again. There was a cafe there, under the crescent shape that formed one side of the Gardens, and she bought a coffee to sit outside.

Contrary to council pensions, which compensated well for a life of service, council redundancies were usually statutory, which meant she would get two and a half months' salary tax-free. That was if they gave it to her, of course. Martin could refuse; he could force her to leave. Her job had never paid amazingly, but it had still been a job, a steady income. Ryan couldn't keep both of them going with his salary. Even as she drank the posh coffee, she was aware that it was a luxury she would soon be unable to afford. Of course, the £2,000 she had spent on Red's funeral would have come in handy. She gave a little laugh at that stunning irony. But the biggest problem was none of this. It was what job she could do now. She had never done anything else.

At times like this, she missed her father. Her mother was the type, even now, to say that things would be alright, that what happened in life generally turned out for the best. When she'd been younger, Shane had sometimes warmed to that sentiment before realising that they were simply platitudes that she wanted to hear and that her mother wanted to give. Her father had been quite different.

Born in Devon, he'd not been from the north of England like her mother, but he seemed to have adopted that stereotype upon settling in the town of Stockport. Those traditions of being tough, outspoken, unsentimental and not suffering fools gladly had found a home in him as far back as she could remember. His rough edges had made them less close, well into her teens, but then she'd recognised the correlation between bluntness and truth and how the resilient objects of nature seldom had a smooth surface. He might tell someone they were a bloody fool, but he would never sit in pity, and he always turned to action.

'Get another job!' he would have said.

'Yeah, but what?'

'What skills do you have?'

'None.'

'Not having that. Pull yourself together.' Then the classic: 'You've got arms and legs. A good brain. Well – a brain.'

They would have sat and itemised her talents. He would have sought out vacancies online, his eyes squinting at the screen, his hands stubbornly traversing the keyboard.

As a man of his generation, he had never had much concern for 'women's matters', and although he would have listened and done his best, the ectopic pregnancy might have been the one thing where he'd have been at a loss. There would have been no action to take, no hope to give, merely empty words of comfort and the awkwardness of ungovernable pain.

'Ryan thinks that he and I have been trying for a baby for over a year now, but what he doesn't know is that I secretly use contraception because I don't want to get pregnant. Now the doctor has suggested IVF, and I'm delaying in every way I can think of.'

Shane could imagine his forehead descending a fraction in wild surprise; even her father had limits to his imperturbability.

'I do have some skills,' she might say finally. 'I'm well organised. I work hard. I have a lot of experience dealing with cases. Piecing together an investigation. Getting to the truth. I like getting to the root of why something has happened.'

He would have grunted. 'Sounds about right.'

For a moment, she smiled to herself; there was some reassurance there, some reservoir of comfort to draw on, whether her father had been gone 10 years or not. It was the one way that the dead persisted for sure: in the memories of those who'd loved them. That generation kept them present, and sometimes the one that followed too, extending a life beyond the curtain fall.

'Perhaps I should join the police. Be a detective. It's the closest fit to what I do.'

'Hm.' The eyes would have been unreadable behind his glasses, blinking, thinking. 'You care about people, Shane. I've always said it. That is your talent.'

The coffee had gone without noticing, and she sipped a dry cup. Opposite her, a group of tourists were talking, hands clutching shopping bags. The street cleaner was scrubbing some obstinate stain from the flagstones, occasionally whistling; he checked his watch once, continued scrubbing and then checked it a second time. Straightening up, he stood beside his bin and waited. Shane heard a clock chime.

With everything the day had brought, she had forgotten that it was the anniversary of the Manchester Arena bombing. She rose and stood, head bowed, for the minute's remembrance of those who'd lost their lives. At the end of Oldham Street was a mural to the dead, the '22 Bees', one for each Mancunian who'd been taken. From where she sat, she could see its distant edge. She could see the striped painted bodies, carrying their pollen, rising in the white, ready to hum and float over the Northern Quarter.

She had known one of the victims, or rather, known her by sight: the daughter of a neighbour six doors down. In her early 20s, perhaps, just starting out. After she'd gone, the marriage had dissolved. The mother had left; the father remained, cutting a lonely, ageing figure. A timely reminder for Shane, under the hushed skies of the city centre, that there was a scale of human trouble and that she firmly occupied neither extremity.

The northern capital had seemed stronger after the attack. Tragedy served to deepen histories, to fortify civic and communal concepts. It had raised the name of Manchester, not lowered it, turning the tables on evil. Could she adopt some of that resilience? Was a city like a person? They were said to have personalities, a character, a life story...

But no, the resilience of a city was the resilience of its people; when horror struck, its buildings were bricks and mortar, nothing more. What persisted were individuals with a common vision for the fundamentals of right and wrong and a resurgent appetite for living. It didn't matter whether they were an office worker or a street cleaner, a penthouse owner or a street-rat. They were all children of Manchester, including Shane. You could keep your London, New York, Paris. This was the greatest city on Earth, dirty and triumphant, as sly as she was noble. Unconquerable.

As the Deceased Affairs officer walked through the Northern Quarter, she spotted the homeless man she'd interviewed after Red's death. He was sitting in exactly the same position as before, by the doors of a Tesco Metro, giving the impression that he hadn't moved in all this time. Once again, he was grateful for the offer of a hot drink, and Shane surprised him by remembering his drink of choice: hot chocolate mocha, three sugars.

The routines with sugar, stirrer and rucksack pocket had not changed; he shivered involuntarily as he gulped down the warm liquid, and a glow settled in his cheeks.

'God bless,' he said. When she stayed put, he added, 'Here, you're that thingy from the council, aren't ya? Did you ever find out what happened to that boy?'

'Yes,' she replied. There was a low brick wall which formed one side of an ornamental flower bed, and this time she sat on it. 'Well,' she said, 'more who he was.'

'And?'

'His name was Red. He was from here. A son of Manchester. We gave him a funeral. A good funeral.'

'A son of Manchester,' he repeated, eyeing her with interest. 'And his thumb? You asked about his thumb before.'

'Hm. I think you were right. He borrowed money for something and then couldn't pay it back. So they came for his thumb.'

'Gambling, were it?' He shook his head. 'Whatever, should have known better. They always come for their money.'

'I think he knew that. It wasn't gambling.'

'What were it then?'

'Something important.'

'More important than a thumb?' An incredulous look.

She nodded.

'Did you find his folks?'

'Yes,' she said, and her face told the man everything he needed to know.

He scratched his cheek. 'Ah. Bet they were a right bunch of cunts, no?'

Shane thought for a moment. 'Yes. Yes, they were.'

He rose and drained the plastic cup. Slung his bag on his back. 'I need to be going,' he said. 'People to see, places to be.'

'Where are you headed?'

'The shelter.'

She walked with him, supporting his arm as he hobbled on his left leg.

'Oh, that's from years back,' in answer to her question. 'Got some kind of flaming cut in it. Turned nasty till it got seen to. It's fine now.'

'How long have you been homeless?'

'I don't count.' Then: 'I was a lad like that Red of yours when I started out.' He paused. 'There was a girl, you know. That he used to hang around with.'

'Gracie.'

Surprise spread across his face. 'Yeah, that's the one. She was quite popular with our lot for a while there. 'Specially the newbies. Became a bit of a voice for them. But then she left town. Heard she passed as well.'

'What was she like?'

'Fire in human form,' he said. 'The reddest hair you've ever clapped eyes on. And she could bite your hand off as soon as look at yer.'

'What's your name?'

'Dennis. Yours?'

'Shane.'

'Shane. That's a lad's name.'

'Not always.'

'Shane, you seem troubled. Like worried.' He fixed his gaze on her, rather like her father used to.

She could have brushed it aside, but she didn't. 'Some decisions to make. To face.'

He nodded. 'Life's a bitch.'

'Any advice?'

'You wanna listen to the likes of me?'

'Your ideas are as good as anybody's.'

'Well,' he said. Whatever you've done, you did what you can, right?'

'I guess so.'

'We're all doing what we can with what we got given.'

'True.'

'So. You know. Take it easy.'

They had reached the shelter. She offered her hand. A little taken aback – as though unused to the custom – the homeless man shook it. They were the same height and studied each other briefly, eye to eye, new assessments going on. Her life was more than giving dignity to the nameless departed; it was good to be reminded of that. She patted his shoulder, and he turned to pass through the front door of the charitable house.

'Good to meet you, Dennis,' she said.

'Likewise.'

Shane retraced her steps to the corner of Oldham Street. She looked up at the old trading exchange, the stout limestone facade, the decorative ledges of another era, the covered entrance where Red's body had been found.

After a minute or so, she sat on the ground. Watching the world, she could have been homeless herself. Nobody stared at the smartly dressed woman occupying the pavement; it was as if she'd been absorbed into the fabric of the metropolis.

The sole way was forward. Like time flowing in its singular direction, making the centuries turn and the generations fall, you had to persevere in your unfolding history. Irresistibly, against pain or suffering, you had to move forward, in the warm chaos, until the last day.

Tonight she would sit and talk with Ryan. She would tell him about her desperate grief, her fears, the truth about the contraception she had used. About their ectopic, the curled up, waiting bee. And she would tell him that she had left the job she'd had since school.

The sun had re-emerged after a morning of being buried, and it lit the Gardens and its sprawling surroundings. It brought more people out, and she saw a boy and a girl, mischief-eyed, dallying with the idea of running through the fountains. To her left, three cashpoints were being prodded; to her right, some lads were chatting in a group four or five strong; in the distance, framed by the overhead tramlines, an elderly couple held the hand of a grandchild, and their heads kept bobbing and turning and looking down at the little girl, solicitously, pleasurably.

As the pigeons launched their circle overhead, a sea of heads glanced up at their rampant noise, then resumed their business. The sea careened gently under the light, silhouetted, moving, alive, living. Mortal shapes as far as the eye could see: the Named and the Nameless. They were all one under the sun.

Perhaps life and death are not opposites, Shane thought. I have no insight into the nature of death; as a living being, I partake in life alone. Perhaps they are two separate essences, elemental, distinct, differing, like peculiar sub-atomic particles, or divergent species – the two species of experience. Until the day I die, I cannot know.

She looked ahead of her. A man was navigating the mill of traffic around him, turning sideways and catching up his feet, but then he caught sight of her stillness and gazed down. The stranger's eyes locked on hers. They were black eyes: full, knowing, never absent in their human way. She saw him reach for his pocket. She raised a declining hand, and he stopped mid-donation. He walked on.

A clamour of voices travelled continuously around the urban space. She recognised in herself the burning need to be in the company of others, of the living: surrounded by her kind. No quietus. Only animus.

She rose from her seat, stepped into the crowd. This is where I belong, she thought.

ROSE

Red and Gracie arrived in the town of Whitby at the end of a three-day journey. All their money pooled was less than £10, so there was no chance of them buying fares. Slow trains, which stopped at every town and village, were less stringent with their ticket checks than the intercity ones, so they travelled to the coast on those; with station stops coming every five to ten minutes, they got off whenever an inspector was coming and waited for the next transport. It was the first time that he had known them to steal. Gracie preferred to characterise it as 'charity' from their fellow passengers in a time of need, even if it was unwitting and at odds with their stares of open disgust.

Days had passed since either one of them had used a shower or put on clean clothes. Gracie smelled of sick; he felt sure the stench of the disused Chinese restaurant, with its burgeoning wildlife and their excrement, clung to him. They slept outside stations when their day's journeying was done. Reaching this other place that the young woman had mysteriously chosen had become their goal. It was more than an escape from the death of their friend and the attention of the authorities. It was an escape from everything, a strange symbol of hope, the pilgrimage of an unspecified faith. Fatigue showed itself in every part of Gracie's body, and she would fall asleep within minutes of settling in her seat. She rested her head against Red's shoulder, and he leaned to receive the weight.

Waiting for them beyond the modest railway station was a view unlike any the young man had seen before. His eye fastened on the rows of tiny boats and their beautiful wooden masts, the red-roofed, white-walled houses built into the hillside, and on its summit, the ancient, dark-stoned abbey. It was the first time he had ever seen the sea. In the harbour, its surface undulated, humbly mirroring the human constructs which crowded its edge. Then, as they walked along the promenade, he could pick out its proper swell, the open ocean, like some other creature altogether: free, proud, contrary. The sun crowned the far, rolling waters.

By now, his eye was accustomed to seeing in any vista the opportunities that it afforded his ilk. He found a place to shelter from the sharp wind and within minutes they were asleep.

Wherever there are people in numbers, there are the Homeless to complement them. The next morning, Red and Gracie spoke to the beggars of Whitby, sitting at one end of a bridge that spanned the harbour, and asked where they might get showered, wash their clothes and have food.

Then they walked through the town and up the steps to the abbey on the hilltop, with its cemetery that overlooked the harbour. It was the most peculiar feeling. With their bags hidden away, they had strolled unencumbered by the waters and could have passed for two muggles on holiday.

They wandered between the gravestones. Bleak monuments to those who had perished in their boats, they were perishing now themselves, at the hands of an unforgiving sea air. There were at least a hundred of them, tilting in their rows: a hundred men who had chosen the mariner's life and its precarious ways. He was aware of Gracie sitting beside him on the bench. Gazing at the grey horizon, Red had a sudden vision of what their own future might be.

There was a home. It was modest, but it was lit, and it was warm. The home was here, or maybe it was in Manchester, perhaps some other spot. The two of them were there, and the whole place was full of happiness, as though happiness might be seen and touched and inhaled. Happiness in the kitchen where the meals were cooked, happiness in the shower room where warmth was on tap in an instant. And he knew with a piercing clarity that such permanent shelter could never be a prison, no matter what Gracie had said. For a prison was not defined by the sum of its four walls and roof but by what happened within them.

At the foot of the hill was a street with tourist shops, and they went in to have a look. As they browsed the postcard stands and picked their way between the shelves of trinkets, Red turned to Gracie and said:

'We should get something. To remember Bart by.'

She emptied her pockets: 70p. He held up a pound between thumb and forefinger. 'We know our budget, then,' he said.

Gracie drew a bookmark from one of the revolving stands. It must have been from a range, but it was the last one. This particular writer was a seller anywhere in the country, it seemed.

Red took it in his hand. The label said £1.65. He handed over the money, and they left.

In the low doorway, he stopped and read the quotation aloud:

What's in a name? That which we call a rose by any other name
would smell as sweet.

Their eyes met for a moment. 'How many homeless people appreciate a good bit of Shakespeare, do you think?'

She smiled. 'Not many.'

'There weren't many like him, though.'

'No,' she said.

'Here,' he said. 'You should have it.'

Gracie took the piece of card. 'He was your friend too.' While Red watched, she tore it in two.

'Thank you,' he said.

They each pocketed a half. The sea light was behind her profile, and he saw, as if for the first time, that there was beauty in her features, a small, doll-like beauty, as if a painter had applied the gentlest of strokes to render a nose, a mouth, those faint eyebrows above her striking amber eyes. Then the redness of the hair above, as vivid and earthy as the leaves that lingered on the hill steps and between the abbey graves.

'You are a rose,' he said.

There was surprise at first in her eyes, and he couldn't tell whether there was pleasure there too. She smiled.

'Watch them thorns, then,' she said.

'Why Whitby?' he asked. Now they had left the tourist shops and were walking down to the muddy-sanded beach which fanned out from the harbour inlet. On the way, they passed a van selling coffee and doughnuts and another selling sticks of rock and other candies. The coffee seller threw some leftover doughnuts into the gutter for the seagulls, and his neighbour started having a go at him.

'Don't throw them scraps. They're bloody vermin.'

'The stuff's stale.'

'You're only encouraging them. You'll be sorry when they start on your fresh stock.'

Gracie looked like she was considering whether to answer Red's question. ''Cos of my dad,' she said. 'He wanted us to come 'ere. Me and,' – there was a definite pause – 'me sister Lisa. But 'e died before we could come. Then everything went bad. I wanted to see the place. Like, wot I missed out on.'

In Gracie's eyes, he read the need to speak. A fragment had been told, like a first cut; the rest would come now, like a tree falling under its own weight. It was the story that Gracie had never shared before: of her father's death, her mother's addiction, a violent stepfather and how her sister was murdered.

'Gracie and Lisa,' she said. 'I were the one with the sad, old name. Me nana named me and then pegged out. She liked Gracie Fields. So I got lumbered wi' it.'

'Not heard of her.'

'She were a singer from ages ago. A Manc, born and bred, but famous all over the world. Me and Lisa. We was thick as thieves, you know. Close like yer wouldn't believe.'

Her mother had been an addict as far back as she could remember, and her father the one who always tried to get her clean. No sooner had he weaned her off one drug than another had her hooked. It was the company she kept; it was boredom; it was something in her that meant she couldn't resist the temptation. He tried to isolate the two children from the constant fallout but inevitably failed: they were there when the ambulances were called or when police turned up at the front door. They heard him crying sometimes when they were supposed to be asleep, having been in bed for hours, whispering with the lights out. In turn, as the elder sibling, Gracie had tried to protect Lisa, and they were inseparable in each other's company.

Then one day, he left. They woke to find their mother cursing and weeping. She promised them with staring eyes that she would look after them herself, that they didn't need him, that he was scum, a loser!

'But wot she didn't know was he'd put a note under me pillow. Said he'd come back for us. And 'e did. We were so excited. I remember we did a little dance right there in the dark. We didn't want to be with 'er, even then. We knew he'd save us.'

For a short time, things settled down, and the sisters lived happily with their father. He planned a fresh start for them; he would take them to Yorkshire, which was where he'd been brought up, in the town of Whitby. But illness overtook him before they could make the move: a cough developed that never abated; he was diagnosed with lung cancer. Treatments failed, and within a few months, he fell into a coma before dying in the hospital.

Their mother regained custody. If it had been an unhappy time for them before, the misery this time was another order of magnitude. The one adult they had ever trusted was gone, and their mother spoke against his memory with a bitter tongue. Her drug-free days were soon over. And then Jamie appeared, the new boyfriend.

'I don't know why 'e were so fucking evil. Right deep inside. I don't know why she let 'im be so evil. It made 'er evil too. And they just picked on Lisa. I didn't get it. Like, why her? And not me? She were too good, I think. Too sweet and kind. They picked on 'er 'cos they knew they could.'

Lisa washed some clothes but forgot to hang them out for drying. Their mother needed little persuasion to lock her in the dark, cramped utility cupboard for two hours. She screamed, whimpered, called out for her lost father. The whole episode inflamed an aberrant pleasure in the two adults; once kindled, it would not be put out. For Gracie, too, it was a turning point, as she feared the dark even more than Lisa did, and that fear kept her mute. It became the first moment of separation between those inseparable sisters.

Humiliation was central to the punishments meted out, and Lisa was made to get on her hands and knees and mop the floor with her hair. They gave her a dog bowl to eat from. When Lisa wet herself the following week, Jamie beat her while their mother egged him on. A shoe was his instrument of choice, and he applied it in sudden bursts of energy. Gracie couldn't bear to watch. She went to her room and waited for Lisa to appear. Hours passed. Once the TV and lights were off and her mother's bedroom door closed, she emerged to unhook the latch on the utility cupboard and set her sister free.

Incidents became too common to count or remember. A padlock was put on the cupboard door. Lisa's imprisonments became more regular; cable ties and cuffs were used to restrain her; a bucket was set up as a toilet; she was left whole days and nights without food or water; when she was released and her thirst so bad, Jamie would make her drink from the bucket.

'She 'ad this beautiful, golden hair. It began to fall out in chunks. She'd wet 'erself. I didn't know if she couldn't 'elp it or if it were some kind of "fuck you" to them. There were bruises all over 'er arms.' Gracie lowered her head. 'They would pinch 'er, punch 'er. They even kicked 'er. Stamped on 'er. They would take 'er wrist and burn it wi' a cigarette. I saw it all. I didn't know wot to do. I 'ad zero trust in the Gimps, teachers, anyone in authority. We saw wot had 'appened when dad died, and the court gave us back to 'er. We shoulda been protected, but they didn't give a shit. I started thinking about killing 'em in their sleep. There was this big carving knife in the kitchen drawer, and I'd stare at it. But the thing is, Red, I weren't brave enough to do it.' Her golden eyes twitched at the relived horrors. Her hands wrung convulsively; her voice rasped with fear. 'I wish I'd been brave enough. Then Lisa would still be 'ere.'

'You can't blame yourself for that.'

'I could see meself holdin' it, stickin' it in their chests. But wot if I messed up? Wot if they didn't die? How were I gunna kill 'em both? And then I did summat really bad. I feel so guilty about it. But the smell was so bad... Lisa hadn't washed for weeks, not brushed her teeth, nuthin'... and I still shared a room with her. One day I had a go at her. Like, a proper, proper go. We started scrapping on the floor. It weren't about her really. I was just so afraid, and it all came out – at the one person it could. I've tried so hard, but I can't forget that. My kid sister needed me, and I fuckin' fought her as hard as I could.'

On the evening that Lisa died, she'd been left to watch a pot of cauliflower cooking on the hob. Soon an acrid smell reached the living room, and the three of them found her standing in the kitchen, watching the thing burn, as though complicit in the act of violence to come. Their mother slung the pot into the sink and turned on the cold water. Steam erupted into the air amid a violent hissing sound. Jamie grabbed Lisa by the arm and threw her against the wall. They heard the terrible crack as the little girl's head hit the whitewashed brick.

'And that were that,' said Gracie. 'One second there, alive; the next second, dead. They went to prison. 'Ope they rot. I hate them both. It'll never bring her back.'

Red didn't know what to say.

'This is why I said to yer before 'bout Darren. Can you imagine the place I was in when I got taken into care? They tried shoving me into therapy. All sorts of crap. But I could barely even speak. He helped me. Talked to me like a normal person. Until I could stand on my own two feet again. It were like wakin' up; that's the only way I can describe it. Comin' back into my body.'

'And then you went onto the streets?'

'I got placed with a foster 'ome. I fuckin' hated it. They weren't bad, the people I were placed with. But I couldn't stand being in a house wi' a family. It all seemed so, I dunno, fake. All this pretend happiness when I knew how bad home could be. I felt sick being in any four walls. So I ran away, took to the streets. Darren were no longer around. I had no way of contactin' him. I were on my own. And then I met B. Glorious, kind, wise B. He asked nuthin' about my past, wanted nowt. 'E were a poor soul himself, all broken up, though he tried to hide it all. Typical that I ended up with another addict. 'E were weak like my mum. But he were good like me dad. 'E were the best of men.'

'Yes, he was.'

'The Street suited me. I knew it after a few days. Swore on me life I'd never leave. I never will,' she added, looking at him with intensity. 'The code was somethin' I came up with after the first week – it simply popped into me head. It weren't supposed to be rules. It were stuff that helped me cope with being 'omeless. The

Street made me who I am.'

They had reached the seafront. Here the benches were made of stone, as wood could not survive the close attention of the elements. The beggars sat.

'I saw 'em,' Gracie said.

'Saw who?'

'Lisa. Me father. When I took the Spice with B, I went to a place. I saw what it were like after death.' She stared at Red. 'I know it were the Spice... I *know* it were the Spice, but it were as real as me seeing you now.'

The young man frowned. 'What did you see?'

'I were with B. We were walking and talking, and we went into this place, and 'e called it the Shadowlands. That name makes it sound bad, but it weren't. He was so happy, and I was so happy. Then I saw me father were there, and Lisa too. They'd come to collect B. I walked with 'im all the way until I 'ad to turn around. And when 'e said goodbye, he told me that our little lives are rounded with a sleep.'

'It's not time for us to sleep yet,' Red commented, studying her. A swell of foreboding, imprecise but malign, rose within him. He thought of his vow to the old man to look after Gracie, and he felt an abrupt fear that he wouldn't be enough. 'You were hallucinating,' he said. 'It was the drugs.'

'I thought yer said death wasn't the end.'

'Hm.'

'Yer never told me why you left 'ome.'

'No.'

'Bet it ain't as good a story as mine.' It was the most morbid piece of humour that he'd ever heard. Gracie's eyes shone with some unknowable energy.

A harsh wind blew across his face as he turned to look at the waves. The first 15 years of his life were a dull tale: he had been on his own most of the time. His parents had been uninterested.

He had found ways to look after and entertain himself; the desire to escape unhappiness had burned in him for years. Then the turning point which even he did not fully understand: the death of a tramp; his arrest; that sudden, vengeful decision to run away...

'Yer parents are self-centred twats,' she said once his story was told. 'You made the right call.'

'Think so?'

'I know so.'

Their attention was drawn to a young family walking past them onto the beach. Insanity to play on the sands in late winter, but they didn't seem to care. The father shouted and kicked the ball, the pet dog barked, the children clamoured.

'Do you think we'll stay here?' he asked. It was the first time the prospect of a joint future had been raised and words given to what it might look like.

'I don't know,' she said. 'It's beautiful 'ere, but...' Her voice trailed off. He knew what she meant. It wasn't Manchester. They shared the white-winged cries of gulls circling the grey-blue above, but the seaside town had a sweet and shallow soul compared to the great mass of buildings, the traffic, the rowdy squalor of the city they'd come from. Was it possible to love the colour of grime and to miss the scents of an urban landscape? It would seem so, as he felt it then.

How long would they wait? When would Bart's body be discovered? Would others in the homeless community notice that they'd gone? Red had no answer to any of the questions.

'What about the code?'

'Wot about it?'

'People will still want it. Need it.'

'The code is dead,' she said.

'Dead?'

'It's worthless. Means eff all. Did the code save B?'

He hesitated. 'No, but it wasn't supposed to.'

'The code makes no difference 'bout what matters. If you died tomorrow, the code wouldn't matter. If I died tomorrow, the code wouldn't matter. Nothing would. No one cares. No one would give a shit. Can't yer see that?'

'Not true,' he said. 'If you... If anything happened to you, it would matter. To me.'

She was silent.

'So if the code is wrong,' he challenged back, 'then the Street isn't shelter from life. She doesn't care about us; there is no shelter. She isn't good; she isn't bad. She doesn't give a shit. Is *that* what you're saying?'

'I didn't say the code is wrong!' The grief of B's death was still raw on her face. 'Wot d'yer want from me?'

'Want? Nothing.'

'No,' she said. 'Don't lie! Yer want us off the streets, in some safe, shitty place with a mortgage.'

He went to speak, but she cut right through him. 'Everyone's always makin' out we need saving. That we're all dyin' to get under a "red roof". Well, I'm not. Fuck that. Wi' fuckin' bells on. Haven't yer twigged yet? A home is a prison. Both of us came from exactly that.'

'It doesn't mean a third home would be.'

'Stop peckin'! Stop makin' me yer charity project. This is where I belong. Where people like me belong. The people who fucked up!'

'Ah, just listen to yourself.'

'I don't want this life you've got in mind. If it's 50 years at the hands of others versus 10 years on the Street, I'll take the Street.'

'And what if it isn't 10 years?' His voice cracked, low, angry. 'What if it isn't even five? What if it isn't one?'

'Then that's the gamble.'

The family on the beach turned at the sound of raised voices. They continued with their game. Red laid a hand on her arm, but she shrugged it off.

'You're making me into yer code. Yer pet project. Well, I don't wanna be. I don't want to be anyone's anything.' The anger rose again. 'Stop tryin' to save me. Yer don't get it. You cannot save me. I am like... like a bent nail. I can't be straightened. I couldn't even save me sister. I couldn't save B. You couldn't neither! How are you gunna save me?'

She went to walk off, but he grabbed her wrist. They sat there, huddled against the wind and a sky that looked like rain.

Then, after what seemed like an age, a curious thing happened: her hand came up and gently held onto his arm. 'I'm sorry,' she said. 'I'm trying. Tryin' not to be horrible. I'm not gunna change my mind. But that's not your fault.'

Red's heart sang wildly for a split second. The warmth of that female touch seemed to irradiate his arm and spread through his entire body. All the misery he had ever known was gathered and suppressed in a single instant under her tiny hand. She was right that life didn't have to be extended to obtain its meaning. Only fleeting. Some illusion of purpose. Some*one* to know the emptiness with. Even for a day.

There was no sun in the sky, no parting of the clouds: a sky of foreboding. And still, he felt burning within him a great, new certainty and that mythical sense of belonging which, he realised now, had existed as a gaping hole within himself. He belonged with her, whatever might happen. To belong: a willing prison.

'Gracie.'

She looked up and smiled, her features captured in a moment of what might be happiness, of reconciliation with the inexplicable past and the unwritten future.

Boldly, the homeless man took the homeless woman's hand: the fingers knitting, his thumb perfectly enveloping hers.

'What's in a name?' he said quietly. 'Everything.'

THE END